Layman's Bible Book Commentary
Leviticus, Numbers, Deuteronomy

LAYMAN'S BIBLE BOOK COMMENTARY

LBBC

LEVITICUS, NUMBERS, DEUTERONOMY

VOLUME 3

Roy Lee Honeycutt, Jr.

BROADMAN PRESS
Nashville, Tennessee

4211-73

ISBN: 0-8054-1173-9

Dewey Decimal Classification: 222.13

Subject headings: BIBLE. O. T. LEVITICUS//BIBLE. O. T. NUMBERS//
BIBLE. O. T. DEUTERONOMY

Library of Congress Catalog Card Number: 78-73278

Printed in the United States of America

Foreword

The *Layman's Bible Book Commentary* in twenty-four volumes was planned as a practical exposition of the whole Bible for lay readers and students. It is based on the conviction that the Bible speaks to every generation of believers but needs occasional reinterpretation in the light of changing language and modern experience. Following the guidance of God's Spirit, the believer finds in it the authoritative word for faith and life.

To meet the needs of lay readers, the *Commentary* is written in a popular style, and each Bible book is clearly outlined to reveal its major emphases. Although the writers are competent scholars and reverent interpreters, they have avoided critical problems and the use of original languages except where they were essential for explaining the text. They recognize the variety of literary forms in the Bible, but they have not followed documentary trails or become preoccupied with literary concerns. Their primary purpose was to show what each Bible book meant for its time and what it says to our own generation.

The Revised Standard Version of the Bible is the basic text of the *Commentary,* but writers were free to use other translations to clarify an occasional passage or sharpen its effect. To provide as much interpretation as possible in such concise books, the Bible text was not printed along with the comment.

Of the twenty-four volumes of the *Commentary,* fourteen deal with Old Testament books and ten with those in the New Testament. The volumes range in pages from 140 to 168. Four major books in the Old Testament and five in the New are treated in one volume each. Others appear in various combinations. Although the allotted space varies, each Bible book is treated as a whole to reveal its basic message with some passages getting special attention. Whatever plan of Bible study the reader may follow, this *Commentary* will be a valuable companion.

Despite the best-seller reputation of the Bible, the average survey of Bible knowledge reveals a good deal of ignorance about it and its primary meaning. Many adult church members seem to think that its study is intended for children and preachers. But some of the newer translations have been making the Bible more readable for all ages. Bible study has branched out from Sunday into other days of the week, and into neighborhoods rather than just in churches. This *Commentary* wants to meet the growing need for insight into all that the Bible has to say about God and his world and about Christ and his fellowship.

BROADMAN PRESS

Contents

LEVITICUS

NUMBERS

DEUTERONOMY

LEVITICUS

Introduction

Experiencing the Lord's presence with his people is the central theme of Leviticus. Set in the plains beneath Mount Sinai (cf. Ex. 19:1 ff.), the book grapples with the question of how the Lord may be present with his people. One part of that answer came in building the tabernacle and establishing the priesthood as prescribed in Exodus 25—40. Now that the ministry and the place of worship had been identified in the book of Exodus, Leviticus addressed the remaining issue, the worshiper. Fundamental to the presence of God described so graphically in Exodus 19:1 is the fact that his holiness is such that only Moses, and later Aaron and the seventy elders, could approach him.

So Israel's question was twofold. Where is the Lord's presence? How could one experience that presence after Israel had left Mount Sinai? These two questions are central to the whole of Israel's worship. They are no less pertinent to every age and person: Where may I be sure of the Lord's presence; how may I experience that presence? So Leviticus is concerned with the Lord's word on how we may dedicate life to him.

The whole of Leviticus revolves around the implications of God's holiness. For ancient persons, and for Old Testament believers more particularly, "holiness," when applied either to God or to persons, stressed the "otherness" of one's being. Such difference related not merely to the superiority of God's knowledge, power, or presence; rather, at the core of his being, God is totally other than humanity. Persons are "holy" because they belong to God. Their lives are characterized by an "otherness" in the sense that they belong to this holy God whose otherness transcends their own being.

Holiness is a way of defining relationship. Neither persons nor objects are holy in themselves. Even utensils used in worship, the altar, and Jerusalem itself were holy. But as inanimate objects, they were amoral, capable of being neither good nor bad, perfect nor imperfect, in the moral connotation of perfection. They were "holy" by virtue of a relationship; they belonged to God and were used in his service.

Yet holiness does not mean to be unapproachable or inaccessible, for either God or persons. God is holy but not incapable of relationship with persons. Persons also are holy but are not incapable of relationships with God's creation. Rather, holiness is a way of relating to, not escaping from, the reality of life and other persons. Leviticus is concerned with leading Israel to a dedication of life which will reflect the reality of God's presence. How may persons experience the holiness of divine presence? In turn, what are the implications for daily life for those who do experience the presence of One who is wholly other than creation or persons? Leviticus is a word from God on the dedication of life, both personal and national.

Title

The English title "Leviticus" identifies the book with those matters of specifically Levitical interest. The Levites themselves are infrequently mentioned (only in 25:32-34), and the book is Levitical in the sense that it is fundamentally concerned with priestly details such as sacrifice, ordination, and the dedication of both personal and national life by embodying a particular life-style. Often described as a manual for priests, Leviticus is far more than merely a priestly manual. Although it does constitute such a manual, its focus is on the worshiper—what the priest is to do as he counsels and directs worship. In this regard it is as much a manual for worshipers as for priests. Portions of the book may have been attached to the shrine as a kind of operating manual for worshipers; or these portions may have been recited for the worshiper by the priest.

The title came via the Septuagint, the Greek translation of the Old Testament, where the Greek title meant "the Levitical (book)." More directly, the Latin Vulgate titled the book "Liber Leviticus." In the Hebrew Old Testament the names of books were most often the first word in the individual books. So, in the Hebrew text, Leviticus is known as "The LORD *called* Moses" (Lev. 1:1). As with the whole of Scripture, the authority and pertinence of Leviticus are grounded in the assumption that what is contained therein is what the Lord "called" or declared. From the beginning Leviticus was identified as a word which the Lord called to Moses, and through him to the worshiping community of faith. The way in which the word of God permeates the structure of the book is a logical extension of the assumption that the book is grounded in the Lord's calling.

The Lord's Word

Leviticus is uniquely a book of Yahweh's word. Thirty-six occurrences of the phrase "The LORD said" throughout the book solidly affirm the priority of the word. These passages are logical extensions of the same phrases in Exodus (cf. 25:1; 30:11,17,22; 31:1,12; 40:1) and form a literary structure which binds the whole of this material into a single entity given at Sinai (cf. Ex. 19:1 to Num. 10:10).

Moses alone is the object of the Lord's speech in thirty-one instances. In each, the reader confronts essentially the same phrase: "The LORD said to Moses." Few if any English translations clarify the play on words within the Hebrew text. For two verbs appear there—to speak and to say. Careful examination of the Hebrew text reveals that the formula is always the same: "And the LORD spoke unto Moses for the purpose of saying." The "word" came to Moses in order that God might "speak." The phrase became sterotyped in biblical Hebrew and came to mean only that "The LORD said." But the actual text is important. The word of God does come to realilty through speaking, but that "word" is always more than merely words.

This pattern is consistent with other Old Testament literature in its distinction between word and speech. Word is the dynamic reality of God present in creative power. On occasion that word comes to reality through words, but on other occasions it comes through other media, apart from words: "There is no speech, nor are there words; yet their voice goes out through all the earth, and their words to the end of the world" (Ps. 19:3-4). Unless a person listens for the word beyond the words of speech alone or of writing he may fail to experience the reality of God as a dynamic, creative, word/event in his world.

Abiding Emphases

What are the central emphases of Leviticus? More significantly, does the book communicate a word from God to contemporary believers? Or is the book merely of antiquarian interest for those concerned with reconstructing the history of Israel's religious practices? The book is of historical interest, for it is important that we know how Israel worshiped and what the conceptions of God were which informed that worship. But Leviticus is more. It can become the medium for the Lord's word to contemporary persons. The book becomes contemporary, a modern word from the Lord, as we experience the dynamic reality of God. As a person responds, he may experience God's word beyond the words of Leviticus, for the Word is always more than words.

Leviticus speaks to so few today because so few believe that God can come to them through and yet beyond the words of another culture and time. But there is a timelessness about the reality of God's Word. Such timelessness means that we experience the reality of that Word in ways which transcend the original words. If we listen, we can hear a word beyond the words of Leviticus. It is that word of God which prophets and apostles experienced, and it is his word which can become operative in our lives as we stand with openness to both Spirit and word in our study of Scripture. And what does such a book continue to say?

First, one word which uniquely characterizes Leviticus is *worship.* The English word came via Middle English, in which it was spelled "worth-ship." Worship is the *proclamation* of the Lord's worth. But worship is more than the proclamation of God's worth. Worship is also *response.* And Leviticus structures patterns for worshipful response to the Lord in areas such as sacrifice, holy days, vows, and offerings. But it also suggests other patterns drawn from its own culture for the appropriate response of persons to the Lord, of the way in which all aspects of one's activity should reflect the worth of God. What a person eats, how he relates to other persons, his attitude toward sexual matters, ethical issues, and cultural practices—these also are suggestive for an appropriate response to the worth of God.

Second, appropriate for a contemporary casualness concerning God, Leviticus affirms the *holiness of God.* A casual attitude toward God in contemporary culture so contemporizes God that popular theology has little understanding of the uniqueness of God. In the process of assuring the approachability of God or the humanity of God, persons conceive him as of the same order as humanity. Stronger, wiser, and growing, God is created in the image of man. For many God becomes the extension of a person's idealism or the rationalization of his emotional needs. Persons popularize and domesticate God so that they are now comfortable in his presence—Isaiah to the contrary (cf. Isa. 6:1 ff.).

But for ancient Israel he was the "wholly other." Neither unapproachable nor inaccessible, he remained the God of holiness whose ultimate being was lost in mystery and wonder. Such an understanding led ancient worshipers to experience awe, wonder, and adoration in the presence of ultimate mystery grounded in God's "otherness." As contemporary persons prone to humanize God so radically as to lose the awesome grandeur of the God beyond us, we need to hear this ancient word on the holiness of God.

Third, in Leviticus one understands Old Testament *sacrifice* and *atonement, priestly function,* and *lay participation.* As such it is a book to be practiced rather than to be read. Forgetting this, we often lose much of the value of the book. For Leviticus is both a priestly and a lay manual for sacrifice and for other aspects of the dedication of life. Leviticus is a blueprint for sacrifice for which the book of Psalms sets the accompaniment. It portrays sacrifice so that the reader beholds its many-faceted character: dedication, expiation, gift, forgiveness, communion. And for the Christian, Leviticus is no less crucial. This book sketches sacrifice and atonement in the finely detailed patterns which set the background for understanding Jesus' life and death. Yet its value for the Christian is more than that of setting Jesus' life in sacrificial retrospect. Leviticus speaks to both Hebrew and Christian about the claim of God upon the whole of life.

Fourth, Leviticus is a book of *practice,* not of theory. It affirms that God can be known and worshiped in practices consistent with one's culture. Inadequate though some practices may be, they can be genuine responses to the reality of divine presence. No one today is likely to fulfill such literal demands of Leviticus as sacrificial acts, attitudes of "uncleanness" toward bodily infirmity or physiological functions not then understood, or clean and unclean animals. But Leviticus speaks to us of the way in which God claims human life in the light of our understanding and culture. Such a word calls on believers to respond as best they can with the only response possible: practices and understanding characteristic of their culture. The Bible does not speak in theoretical terms of worship. Rather, it speaks of God's call to all persons to respond in light of the understanding common to the times in which they live. Better to practice with imperfection than to theorize with perfection.

Fifth, Leviticus presupposes a thoroughly *religious interpretation of life.* No area of human life rests outside the bound of God's care. Nor is any facet of human existence void of the possibility of dedication. The totality of life is sketched as the arena of commitments. God's people are to live in holy relationship both to him and to one another. As that part of Leviticus known as the "Holiness Code" suggests (Chap. 17—26), the totality of human relationships is shaped by the fact that the person belongs to the Lord. No facet of life is "common," for it is all "holy" in the sense that life belongs to God and is to be dedicated to him. For the ancient Israelite there was no troubling decision, as for some, of determining what part of life was holy and what part common. With open and joyful hearts they could affirm, do all to the glory of God.

The Lord's Word for Dedicating Life Through Sacrifices

1:1 to 7:38

Sacrifice was one of the six Levitical means of dedicating life. It was predicted on the assumption that God is wholly other than persons, yet not unapproachable. It further presupposed that the worshiper was intimately related to the sacrificial gift and that sacrifice did not operate as an act apart from one's spirit of dedication. When offered with sincerity, sacrifice became an experience not unlike Jacob's ladder, bearing two-way traffic from earth to heaven, from heaven to earth.

Studies in the origins of sacrifice suggest that central to the act were appeasing the deity, seeking the deity's favor, or even providing nourishment to the deity through the food sacrificed. More probably, sacrifice reflected one of three origins, and perhaps a combination of each. In earliest form sacrifice constituted a *gift* to the deity, for in giving the gift one gave oneself. Or sacrifice established *communion* between the deity and the worshiper. Also, sacrifice released *life*—whether the life of the worshiper to the deity or the life of the deity for the worshiper. Each of these motivating factors manifested itself at some point in Israel's numerous sacrifices: gift, communion, and release of life. The Lord's continuing word for worshipers is one which affirms that dedication is both achieved and manifested through sacrifice, whether ancient or modern.

This section of Leviticus (1:1 to 7:38) is a manual for sacrifice, not unlike a "pastor's manual" used by some ministers as a guide for conducting weddings, funerals, baptisms, and communion or the Lord's Supper. Given the development of writing in ancient Israel, a copy of that material may have been attached to the shrine for the guidance of both worshiper and priest. Or the priest may have maintained the prescriptions for sacrifice through oral transmission. However available, the stipulations guided both lay and priestly person, with the earlier section for the guidance of the laity (1:1 to 6:7) and the latter for the priests (6:8 to 7:38).

A Lay Manual for Offering Sacrifice (1:1 to 6:7)

The role of laity in Old Testament worship, and especially in sacrifice, is a feature too often forgotten. For example, this section is best described as "a lay manual for sacrifice." More significant than the provision of such a manual for lay persons, however, is the involvement of laity in the rituals of sacrifice. So much is this the case that one must take both the instructions for the laity and the instructions for the priests together in order to create a complete pattern of sacrifice. As only one illustration, to understand the full ritual of the peace offering, for instance, one should consider the instructions for the lay person (3:1-17) as well as those for priestly instruction (7:11-36).

Background Information

These verses introduce the book of Leviticus with the intent of binding the book to what has preceded while identifying what follows as the commanding word of the Lord (v. 2). The phrase "The LORD spoke to Moses" occurs thirty-six times in Leviticus and nine times in Exodus 25—40. Such usage in both books is consistent with the fact that the Sinai narrative extends from Exodus 19:1 through Numbers 10:10 and was written in the form of the Lord's words to Moses for Israel, given at Mount Sinai.

Grounded in the authority of God, Moses' words to the people affirmed the priority in sacrifice of "cattle from the herd or from the flock" (cf. Gen. 4:1-16). The cereal offering described in chapter 2 is likely a later development than the animal sacrifice but has been incorporated into the list of normative sacrifices in Israel. So even in Israel there was later reinterpretation of the Lord's will for differing situations, and that without abandoning his original intention. It seems clear that animal sacrifices had priority in Israel, probably reflecting the seminomadic character of a people who tended cattle and flocks. Cereal sacrifices emerged under the influence of an agrarian culture following settlement in Canaan. But they emerged in a manner consistent with the original intent for sacrifice. The form of worship may change as long as the content remains consistent with its intended character. This can also be extended to other areas of divine will and human action as God's will is reinterpreted in light of emerging cultural patterns which do not alter the central intention revealed by God.

"Any man" (v. 2) is generic and translates the word meaning "mankind." Although restricted by the larger context to Israelites in covenant with the Lord, as opposed to every human being, the word might also be translated "any person." Had the writer intended an individual man, the vocabulary was available in biblical Hebrew. Worship was male oriented in Israel, with wives and children included holistically through the sacrifice by the male head of the household. But the word is not equivalent to the English word "man," as opposed to woman, since the word literally means mankind.

Three Types of Sacrifices (1:3 to 3:17)

First among the instructions provided the laity were stipulations for offering three fundamental sacrifices: *burnt offering* (1:1-17), *cereal offering* (2:1-16), and *peace offering* (3:1-17). The character of sacrifice in Israel fluctuated through the centuries, and the present listing (1:1 to 7:38) probably dates to the postexilic period when the worship life of Israel was fixed in written form much as we now have it in Leviticus. In this process of development one witnesses a practice not unlike the continued silverplating of a vessel. The original shape of the vessel remains clearly delineated, but the overlay of silver from later periods of time produces additional layers which can no longer be disengaged from the original. So in the description of sacrifices, earlier concepts and practices have been overlaid by later practices.

First, the *burnt offering* (1:3-17) had multiple though not unrelated purposes: that the worshiper "may be accepted before the LORD" (v. 3), that the offering shall "make atonement for him" (v. 4), and that the Lord might be pleased (v. 9). Although forgiveness is inherent in the connotation of "atonement," this is not the primary purpose of the sacrifice. In early Israel the burnt offering was the gift offering by the head of household (cf. Gen. 4:4) or by a person like Noah following his deliverance (Gen. 8:20-22). Abraham's near-sacrifice was a "gift offering" signifying the total giving of oneself to the Lord. Laying his hands on the sacrificial animal, the worshiper fully identified himself with the sacrifice (v. 4). In the *complete* burning of the sacrifice (hence the name "*whole* burnt offering") the entirety was given to the Lord, symbolizing the complete self-giving of the worshiper. Thus the sacrifice acknowledged the intuitive response of persons to the Lord, together with the dedication of life characteristic of personal response to God.

"Burnt offering" translates a word which means to go up and may refer to that which goes up to the altar or that which goes up from the altar to God, with the latter the more likely. The entire sacrifice was burned upon the altar and none was eaten by the participants, as was provided in other types of sacrifice. The entire sacrifices offered by fire ascended to the Lord, for whom it was "a pleasing odor" (v. 9).

The role of the lay person was far reaching in the ritual of sacrifice, with only the most holy aspects of the ritual reserved for the priests. The lay person brought the sacrifice to the door of the sanctuary (v. 3), laid his hands on the head of the animal, thus identifying himself with it (v. 4), and then killed the sacrifice (v. 5). After the priest(s) had thrown the blood against the altar (v. 5) the lay person skinned the animal ("flay") and cut it into pieces (v. 6). Then the priests arranged the fire and laid the pieces upon the altar (vv. 8-9). The blood uniquely belonged to God, for the "life" was the blood (cf. Lev. 17:14). Hence, it could not be offered to God. It could only be returned to God by the priest, who had assumed a state of "holiness" which permitted him to deal with so hallowed a reality as blood. Again, because of the holiness of the sanctuary, only the priests could arrange the fire and the animal on the altar, as well as cleanse the "unclean" portions of the animal, the entrails and its legs (v. 9).

The concluding instructions for the ritual of burnt offering are significant for reasons of equality. If one is unable to offer a sacrifice from the cattle (vv. 3-9), he may offer from the flock (vv. 10-13) or from birds (vv. 14-17). The point is clear: No one was denied access to sacrifice through the lack of possessions or wealth. Although lacking the grandeur of cattle, either flocks or birds were available to all, except in the most unusual of circumstances. As in every generation, the sacrificial spirit was unencumbered by physical or material possessions. Of ancient and modern worshipers the word is the same: "Whosoever will, let him come."

Second, the *cereal offering* (2:1-16) served as a "pleasing odor" to the Lord (vv. 2,9,12) and had no other purpose specified in Leviticus. The Hebrew word means a gift or present, and in later Israel it suggested any "gift" of nonanimal and vegetable type. Earlier, however, the sacrifice had the character of a meal—hence the term "meal" or "meal offering" in some translations (KJV).

The prohibition of leaven (v. 4) was common to Old Testament ritual, and the inclusion of honey in the prohibition was related to the fermentation of fruit-honey, which is probably intended. Although neither leavened bread nor fruit-honey was acceptable for an offering on the altar (vv. 4,11), both could be brought as an offering for the sanctuary to be consumed by the priests (v. 12).

The requirement that cereal offerings contain salt and the specific reference to "the salt of the covenant" indicate the way in which covenants were sealed with salt, a most valuable commodity in ancient times. Although the practice is not widely documented in the Old Testament, there are traces of a covenant ceremony sealed with salt, which is described in Exodus as "pure and holy" (Ex. 30:35; cf. Num. 18:19; 2 Chron. 13:5; Ezra 4:14). That salt was necessary for sacrifice is further implied in the items provided the priests of the postexilic era (cf. Ezra 6:9). As Ronald Clements has suggested, "As leaven symbolized what was unacceptable to God, so salt symbolized what made offerings acceptable to him." Salt was a symbol both of friendship and communion and so sheds light on the characterization of Jesus' disciples as "the salt of the earth" (Matt. 5:3). Further, "as salt made an offering pleasing to God, so Christians in the world are to make it acceptable to God." [1]

So the cereal offering was offered as a spontaneous expression of gratitude to God, with no particular requirement specified for its time or frequency. Whoever was willing might make such a gift. And the gift came from the everyday activity of the home; flour or cakes baked in the oven (v. 4), on a griddle (vv. 5-6), or in an earthenware pan (v. 7). For the dedication of life expresses itself in so simple a gift as this and need not wait on the grandeur of more impressive sacrifices.

Third, the *peace offering* (3:1-17) is the last of the fundamental sacrifices prescribed for the worshiper. "Peace" in the plural occurs only in connection with offering or its synonymn. The word goes back to a root word which means whole or complete. In this instance "peace" refers to the wholeness of community created through sacrifice. Such wholeness was inherent in designating a portion of the sacrificial animal for a communal meal, shared by one's family and friends (cf. 7:11-38). The sacrifice marked a time of joy and celebration focusing on wholeness of relationships. One may appropriately speak of it as a "communion meal," which affirmed the bonds that related one to the Lord.

Beyond the words of early Israelite culture, God's commanding word still comes. It does not demand that one respond according to the cultic practices of ancient Israel. But it comes as a Word beyond the words of that culture to affirm the propriety of dedication through the complete giving of self to God (burnt offering), the spontaneous celebration of God's goodness through the common events of life (the cereal offering), and the joyous affirmation of the community which one experiences with both God and persons in the covenant (peace offering).

Seven Categories of Offenses Requiring Sin and Guilt Offerings (4:1 to 6:7)

This section consists of kinds of offenses that require either a sin offering or a guilt offering. On occasion the sin offering is specified (4:2,13,22,27) while in other instances the guilt offering is demanded (5:14,17; 6:1). In some cases the terminology is ambiguous, used synonymously: "bring his *guilt offering* to the LORD for the sin which he has committed, a female from the flock, a lamb or a goat, *for a sin offering*" (v. 6, author's italics). What is the distinction between the two sacrifices?

First, the original distinction between these sacrifices appears to have been lost and the two are for general purposes now used interchangeably (cf. 5:5-6). For example, the description of the ritual appears only for the sin offering, with no effort to prescribe the details of the guilt offering. Second, the original meaning of the words are related to "guilt" or to become guilty, and "sin" or to sin. Although the basic meaning of "sin" here is to "miss the mark," we are not justified in ascribing a more active mood to sin and a more passive mood to guilt, much as we might speak of "sins of commission and sins of omission." For example, sin offerings are prescribed for "unwitting sins" (4:1), thus excluding overt knowledgeable actions by the worshiper. In this instance etymology alone cannot adequately distinguish the religious and theological distinctions between the two.

Third, sin offerings may have referred originally to special times of consecration or purification, while guilt offerings were offered to atone for later, specific sins. Fourth, the distinction between the two may be found in the fact that guilt offerings included the provision for indemnification or reparation for the sin. See 5:16 and 6:4. So far as the manner of offering, the sacrifice, and the forgiveness achieved, there was no distinction between the two sacrifices. Both were extensions of the peace offering previously described (cf, 3:1-17). The primary distinction between these two and the peace offering was the way in which the priests manipulated the blood in the sin offering (and apparently in the guilt offering as well, cf. 4:5-7,16-18). In each the role of the lay person remained significant. He brought the animal to the sanctuary, laid his hands on it, and slaughtered it.

By a striking use of the word for soul as a personal pronoun, the writer/editor isolated seven instances which required sin offerings and guilt offerings. Only once previously in Leviticus had this word been used (cf. 2:1), but in this section there are seven usages (cf. 4:2; 5:1,2,4,15,17,21; 6:2).

Violation of the Lord's command (4:1-35).—All of chapter 4 focuses on the unwitting violation of the Lord's command by the priests (vv. 1-12), the congregation (vv. 13-21), the ruler (vv. 22-26), and the people of the land, "the common people" (RSV, vv. 27-35). For each group the sacrifice required was less demanding, moving in descending scale from the priests to the common people. As previously specified, provision was made for all levels of socioeconomic station.

Each offense had in common the fact that the sin was "unwitting" and was directed against "any one of the things which the LORD has commanded not to be done" (vv. 1,13,22,27). These were sins of commission, committed in violation of some command of the Lord. Such overt sin, however unwitting, required the sin offering for atonement.

Unwitting sin involved unknown infringements of ritual prescriptions of one type or another, and in this regard Clements cites Jonathan's breach of the vow made by his father Saul (cf. 1 Sam. 14:24-26). But unwitting sin also included sin without premeditation or with no intent of sinning. Such meaning is clarified by the reference to sinning "with a high hand" (Num. 15:30), which suggests sin with deliberate intent. For such willful and flagrant disobedience there was no sacrifice. As in the case of David following the sin involving Uriah and Bathsheba, there remained no adequate sacrifice. Only "a broken spirit; a broken and contrite heart, O God, thou wilt not despise" (Ps. 51:17). But there is a sacrifice for relationships broken through unwitting sins, even when they violate the command of God (4:1-36).

Withholding testimony (5:1).—Although the next four offenses comprise a single, larger configuration of offenses related to guilt through negligence, the fourfold use of the word for "soul" (KJV) or "any one" (RSV) suggests the separate treatment of each violation. A faithful witness in the court of law was a primary concern in ancient Israel (cf. Deut. 19:15-21) and is the focus of the present offense.

Uncleanness by contact (5:2-3).—For ancient persons everything was divided into ritually "clean" and "unclean" categories. At times these distinctions were grounded in mystery itself. For example, "in sexual intercourse (2 Sam. 11:11), birth (Lev. 12), and death (Num. 6:6) potent and mysterious forces are at work, and purification rituals are almost universally associated with these phenomena. Anything repulsive, abnormal, or distorted was likely to be regarded as unclean." [2] Self-preservation was also operative in laws of clean and unclean. Anything that stood outside the direct realm of God, such as other deities or demons, was "unclean." Nonhuman powers hostile to persons in covenant with the Lord were also "unclean," as were animals, foods, and practices of non-Israelite source. So, if any person violated the laws of "clean and unclean" by touching an unclean thing, whether nonhuman or human, he had sinned against the Lord; and a sin offering was required.

Rash oaths (5:4-13)—Oaths and vows were taken seriously in Israel. Once made they must be fulfilled, or the person was guilty of sinning against the Lord. Perhaps it was this seriousness that led the writer of Ecclesiastes to say: "When you vow a vow to God, do not delay paying it; for he has no pleasure in fools . . . It is better that you should not vow than that you should vow and not pay" (Eccl. 5:4-5). Consideration for persons of lesser means is exemplified here, as in previous passages. Normally the sacrifice was a lamb or a goat, but if this was not possible one could offer "two turtledoves or two young pigeons." For those in dire straits, flour might be substituted for the turtledoves or pigeons. But since the offering was for sin, the flour could not have the oil and frankincense specified for the cereal offering (cf. 2:2,4 ff.; 5:11). In this instance, and for the first time in the list of offenses, confession was presupposed prior to offering the sacrifice.

Breach of faith (5:14).—With the breach of faith concerning holy things, new elements emerge in the list of offenses. For example, the writer prescribed a guilt offering, not a sin offering. There was also an assessed value ascribed to the sacrificial animal (5:15,18; 6:6). This was in effect an assessment levied by the priest. Additionally, in the case of a breach of faith against holy things, the worshiper not only brought a ram of set value; but he also made restitution for what he had done. He was fined by adding "a fifth to it" and giving it to the priest (v. 16*b*). So forgiveness through sacrifice alone was inadequate.

Disregarding the Lord's instructions (5:17-19).—This case is much like the violation of the Lord's command discussed earlier in chapter 4. There are, however, significant additions. For example, a guilt offering was required in the present instance, a sin offering in the previous legislation. Perhaps the commands developed in different parts of Israel, at various worship centers. Or they may have developed at different periods of time. However one may explain the difference, the former required a sin offering (4:1 ff.), while the present demanded a guilt offering (5:17). But there is a most significant difference. The guilt offering required a ram without blemish, and the value of the ram varied in relationship to the "price for a guilt offering" established by the priest as though sacrifices were graduated in value.

Breach of faith with a neighbor (6:1-7).—In addition to restoring what was taken (v. 5), the sinner was required to add a fifth of its value to the reparation and give it to the person wronged. Again, one sees a noble and exemplary ideal. It is not adequate to seek the forgiveness of God and forget the injustices done to one's neighbor. An interpretation of forgiveness in terms of God that leaves unresolved the disruption with one's brother is false to the biblical ideal. Stated otherwise, forgiveness is not a license to sin but an avenue to right relationship with God and other persons.

The seven kinds of offenses which required a sin/guilt offering to initiate forgiveness shows a wide range of emphases. Some were ritual, as in the case of laws of uncleanness (5:2-3) and the breach of faith concerning holy things (5:14-16). Others related to unstated areas in which a person might have violated the will of God expressed through prohibitions (4:1-35; 5:17-19). But there remain offenses which illustrate the manner in which ethical conduct within the community of faith was integrated into ritual. Such an emphasis reaffirms the assumption that there are three necessities for worship: a body of belief, a system of ethics, and a means to celebrate the joy of one's faith. To withhold testimony (5:1), to make a rash oath (5:4-13), or to breach one's faith with a neighbor through robbery, abuse of property, or personal gain through oppression (6:1-7)—each of these antisocial acts also leads persons away from God. This section of the book portrays the integrated fabric of Israel's life-style, a fabric which thoroughly meshed religion and ethics, faith and action.

A Priestly Manual for Offering Sacrifices (6:8 to 7:38)

This section forms a manual for instructing priests in the offering of various sacrifices. With the exception of the consecration offering, each sacrifice is clearly identifiable: burnt offering (6:8-13), cereal offering (6:14-23), sin offering (6:24-30), guilt offering (7:1-10), and peace offering (7:11-38). As in the case of the manual for lay persons, the priestly manual was intended as a practical "how-to" guide for offering sacrifice. Whether in written form and appended to the shrine, or orally transmitted generation by generation, the manual was a functional guide for the priestly office.

Burnt Offering (6:8-13; Heb. 6:1-6)

The purpose of the offering is unchanged, as is the participation of the lay worshiper. The only additions in 6:8-13 not found in 1:3-17 are the following instructions specifically related to the priests: The burnt offering was to be on the hearth all night, specified dress was designated for the priest while removing the ashes and carrying them to a "clean" place outside the camp (vv. 9-11). The fire on the altar was not to go out, day or night, and it was assumed that the burnt offering was an established sacrifice offered daily (vv. 12-13). The latter stipulation probably reflects a time late in the life of Israel when the burnt offering was not only a personal sacrifice but national in scope and offered daily on behalf of the community.

Cereal Offering (6:14-23)

This offering is different from the baked goods brought from the home (Lev. 2:1-16). The present instructions provide for an offering which the priest ("Aaron and his sons") offered in connection with ordination (v. 20). Although not technically a cereal offering by the populace, the sacrifice is so much like the traditional offering that we may legitimately characterize it as a "cereal offering." The fine flour of the offering was divided by time, with half offered in the morning and the other half in the evening (v. 20). Apparently the flour was first baked on a griddle "like a cereal offering" (v. 21).

Sin Offering (6:24-30)

Here also the instructions are restricted to priestly action, and the previous information for lay and priestly participation is presupposed. For example, the priest who offered the sin offering could eat the offering, sharing it with "every male among the priests."

Holiness, like uncleanness, was thought to have been contagious; it could be transferred through contact. Hence, laws governed the cleansing of garments stained through sacrificial blood (v. 27), and even vessels were either destroyed as in the case of an earthen pot (v. 28) or in the case of a bronze vessel scoured and rinsed in water (v. 28). The mysterious areas of both the holy and that which was taboo could harm one unless appropriate precautions were taken. Both were laden with power, as though with an electrical charge. Hence, people were prevented from ascending Sinai (Ex. 19:24), and Uzzah died when he inadvertently touched the ark to steady it (2 Sam. 6:6-7). Also, when captured by the Philistines, the ark wrought havoc in every city in which they placed it. Such ideas are far removed from contemporary understandings of the holiness of God and its implications, and rightly so. But inherent in those ancient practices was a reverence for the mystery and power of God which every generation would do well to emulate.

Guilt Offering (7:1-10)

Now indistinguishable in form from the sin offering, the guilt offering had no unusual features other than those mentioned in 5:14 to 6:7. Indeed, "the guilt offering is like the sin offering, there is one law for them" (7:7). Although this statement may apply only to the distribution of the offering to the priests, it also succinctly states their synonymous character. These instructions do, however, make additional provisions about not only the guilt offering but the burnt offering and the cereal offering. The priest received as his portion a share of the sacrificial offerings.

Consecration Offering (7:11-27)

Although the form of the sacrifice was essentially a peace offering, and it is so described in verse 11, the stipulations define the occasion for the offering as thanksgiving (v. 12), a vow, or a freewill offering (v. 16). This, and especially the fact that the text specifically lists six offerings among which one was a consecration offering, forces us to

consider the possibility that this offering has so specific a function
as to identify it as a special consecration offering, despite the fact
that in form it is a peace offering.

Earlier stipulations for the peace offering (3:1-17) focused only on
the animal sacrifice, whether an animal from the herd or from the
flock. The priestly manual provided for the addition of unleavened
cakes mixed with oil, wafers, and cakes of fine flour (v. 12). In essence,
if the occasion which prompted the sacrifice was thanksgiving, a combination of the cereal offering (2:1-16) with the peace offering (3:1-
17) was demanded. Also, it was specifically provided that the offering
should be eaten on the day of the offering, leaving nothing until morning (v. 15). This suggests that this was a communion meal. The exception to this was the occasion of a vow or freewill offering, in which
case the food could be eaten on successive days as specified in verses
16-18.

Peace Offering and Summary (7:28-38)

As suggested earlier, the peace offering was foundational for a series
of other sacrifices, among which were the sin/guilt offerings and the
consecration offering on the occasion of thanksgiving, vows, or freewill
offerings. The unique addition provided by verses 28-36 is the stipulation providing the priest his portion of the sacrificial animal. This
was consistent with the principle that those who ministered at the
altar should receive their livelihood thereby.

As we review the Lord's word for dedicating life through sacrifice
(1:1 to 7:38), we are impressed with the tedious manner in which
even the finest details of sacrifice were specified. Yet two considerations should remain clearly in focus. First, as suggested in the introduction, Leviticus is a book of practice, not of theory. It structured the
worship of God according to the culture of the day. In so doing it
utilized practices no longer incumbent upon contemporary worshipers. But in the process Leviticus embodied foundational understandings of the nature and character of God which every generation should
comtemplate. Although the theological substructure beneath the stipulations on sacrifice is not isolated, and explanations for sacrifices
are not always given, the interpreter of the book should probe for
those foundations in seeking to experience the Word of God in a
contemporary setting.

Second, we should remember that sacrifices were accompanied in worship by psalms. Frequently the psalm indicated why the sacrifice was offered (cf. Ps. 116:17-19), while at the same time affirming the spirit which accompanied the sacrifice. So, in reading Leviticus, we have but one part of the worship experience, however valued that may have been. Before judging the individual stipulations in Leviticus, the reader needs to know the psalm that accompanied the sacrifice. Indeed, legitimate judgment of the abiding worth of the stipulations on sacrifice could come only after having experienced the worship experience, which cannot now be recovered. As there are many parts in a symphony, so the stipulations of Leviticus are but one part of the worship experience. Thus, the book is a single score, not the full symphony.

The Lord's Word for Dedicating Life Through Ministry
8:1 to 10:20

Grounded in the biblical understanding of the holiness of God, the priestly ministry emerged through persons whose ministry mediated the presence of God. Representing the people before God and God before the people, the priestly minister remained throughout the history of Israel the central worship leader. But the role of priest in Israel was more than that of worship leader in sacrifice coupled with praise, lamentation, and intercession. The priest was also the teacher in Israel, the custodian of law, and the arbiter of new cases for which current laws were not applicable.

Fundamental to the ministry of the Israelite priest was the biblical conception of holiness. As with sacrifice, so with priesthood—the holiness of God affirmed his otherness. Such otherness did not mean inaccessibility but presupposed that God could be approached under the leadership of persons consecrated to serve as mediators. In one sense the priest was an interpreter—not of language, but of the holiness of God. Stated figuratively, he functioned like a transformer which takes high-voltage electricity from a power line and steps it down so that it can be used in various ways, ranging from electric lights and kitchen appliances to a doorbell or a child's electric train. As such, a transformer enables a person to appropriate high voltage current and use it in ways to meet his need and ability to assimilate the energy. He had access to the holiness of God, characterized by unbelievable power. The priest transformed God's holiness through symbols and rituals to enable persons to appropriate his presence at a variety of levels.

The Commanding Word (8:1-3)

The command to ordain the priests and the stipulations which were to govern that ordination appeared in the Lord's speech to Moses recorded in Exodus 29:1-46. The commandments concerning the building of the tabernacle (Ex. 25:1 to 27:21) had already been fulfilled (cf. Ex. 35:1 to 40:38). It now remained for Israel to ordain the priestly leaders responsible for the tabernacle (Ex. 35:1 to 40:38) and for administering the sacrifices earlier prescribed (Lev. 1:1 to 7.38).

For the tenth time in Leviticus the phrase "The LORD said to Moses" appears and authenticates the contents as God's word for the believing community. The specific actions required and the list of elements specified for ordination reflect the prior statement before Sinai (cf. Ex. 29:1-46). This included assembling Aaron and the congregation together with the holy garments, anointing oil, the bull for the sin offering, two rams for the burnt offering and the dedication offering, plus the basket of unleavened bread. Although the garments are not described in detail, each part conveyed symbolic meaning and is discussed carefully in Exodus. Priestly ordination was grounded in the purposes of God, and both the ritual of ordination and the garments were rich with symbolic meaning.

Ordaining a Ministry (8:4-36)

As early as Genesis 1 the Old Testament focuses on the pattern of divine word and obedient response. God commanded concerning creation; then one reads the response "and it was so." There is a divine pattern conveyed through the use of "word" which stands behind creation. So also in Israel's worship there is a divine pattern which stands behind tabernacle (Ex. 35:1 to 40:38) and priesthood (Lev. 8:1-36). Ordination is the fulfillment of a pattern grounded in the purposes of God.

Cleansing through ritual washing (8:4-9).—Ceremonial cleansing through ritual washing is a universal characteristic of world religions and was an especially important part of Israel's worship. The laver which stood in the court of the tabernacle, and later the Temple, symbolized the cleansing of the priest prior to entering the presence of God. Later the entire body was bathed, especially proselytes in the era prior to the New Testament. The baptism of John the Baptist reflected comparable practices in Judaism. Christian baptism enfused those practices with new theological perspective and symbolism as the church used baptism as the central symbol for entrance into the new faith. Only one who is "clean" can enter the presence of God. How such "cleanness" may be achieved varied from one era to another and often was subject to debate. But there was no debate concerning purity as a prerequisite to the presence of God.

Consecration through anointing (8:10-13).—Anointing with oil consecrated both persons and nonhuman objects to the Lord. Just as the fat of animals was holy and could not be eaten by persons in Israel (Lev. 7:22-26), so the oil of the olive was appropriate for consecration ceremonies. "Anoint" in Hebrew gave rise to the English word Messiah, although anointing as a ritual was a widespread and general means of dedicating persons and objects to the Lord. For example, Aaron anointed the altar and the utensils (v. 11) to consecrate them to the Lord. Kings were also anointed, as were the priests.

Forgiveness through a sin offering (8:14-17).—The stipulations of the sin offering were described in Leviticus 6:24-30, and the focus of the present passage is on the purpose of that sacrifice. First, the altar in its entirety, from the upper projections or "horns" to the base, had atonement made for it. Such actions suggests that "atonement" involved not only forgiveness but consecration. Placing their hands on the head of the bull had identified Aaron and his sons with the sacrificial animal. Symbolically identified with the sacrifice, they experienced the forgiveness of God for sin. Those who minister on behalf of God and persons must first experience divine forgiveness.

Dedication through a burnt offering (8:18-21).—Total dedication is required of worship leaders as of all worshipers, and the burnt offering symbolized the total giving of self to God. Although the original stipulation referred to "atonement" (Lev. 1:4), the primary function of that sacrifice appears to have been the dedication of life. As the sacrifice was totally consumed on the altar (hence the term "whole burnt offering" sometimes used), so the worshiper who was identified with the animal through the laying on of hands committed himself totally to the Lord. The sacrifice assured that one "may be accepted before the LORD" (1:3) and was "a pleasing odor to the LORD" (1:9). Ministry on behalf of God and persons requires the total giving of self, just as it requires forgiveness.

Ordination through a peace offering (8:22-30).—Although this sacrifice is not designated "peace offering" in the text, its basic features are so like that offering (7:11-36) as to justify this identification. It may be that this offering was the "consecration offering" included in the list of six sacrifices in chapter 7. The ram was identified as "the ram of ordination," and in this ceremony the office was formalized. The Hebrew phrase for "ordain" is suggestive: "fill the hand." Perhaps the phrase referred to the functions committed to the priest, but it is significant that ordination was linked to the tasks and responsibilities of office. So "ordination" means "a filling"—that is, of the hand in ministry.

The use of the blood was also significant in the ritual of ordination. Before throwing the blood on the altar, as was customary, Moses placed blood on three parts of Aaron's body: his right ear, his right thumb, and his right "great toe." For most persons the right side is the one of strength used primarily in one's work. Moses consecrated the priest's ear because he heard the voice of God, his right thumb because of the ministry he performed, and his right foot because of the sacred places where he ministered. Persons today have a holistic view of the body which was lacking in ancient Israel. In that culture psychological functions were ascribed to physical parts of the body. So the eye, ear, tongue, hand, foot, etc., were understood to function autonomously and could be addressed as persons. The ritual of ordination reflects this belief. Translated into our terms, consecration means that the whole of our functions should be dedicated to the Lord.

Communion through a common meal (8:31-36).—The peace offering was a sacrifice which celebrated the community established between God and the worshiper, as between the worshiper and other persons. This was symbolized by sharing a common meal which included priests and other friends (cf. Lev. 7:11-36). So the ordination ritual also concluded with the celebration of community and the sharing of a common meal (v. 31).

In summary, there is no obligation for contemporary believers to implement the ancient ritual of ordination according to the cultural patterns that prevailed in ancient Israel. But there are enduring principles which inhere in the obedient response of Israel in ordaining priests. First, the commanding word receives obedient response as persons discover through ministry in its broadest definition another avenue for the dedication of life to the Lord. Second, before one can minister to/for other persons, there are prerequisites much like the seven stages of the ordination ritual: the *cleansing* of one's life that one may minister as a "clean" person, *consecration* of oneself to a holy task, the *forgiveness* of one's sin, the total giving of oneself in *dedication*, filling one's hand with the *tasks of ministry*, and *communion* through common participation with others in the work of God.

Experiencing the Glory of God (9:1-24)

Following the seven days required for the ordination of the priests, Moses led the people through a series of four sacrifices to experience the glory of God. Chapter 9 is bounded, first, by the promise of that glory (9:6). Then the fulfillment of that promise is affirmed at the close of the same chapter: "And the glory of the LORD appeared to all the people." "Glory" was one of those indirect ways of speaking of God at a time in the development of Israel's faith when God himself was so venerated that his name could not be used directly. Often glory was symbolized by light (Ex. 13:21) and the presence of God through fire (cf. Ex. 3:2; Judg. 13:20). At the conclusion of the sacrifices, "fire came forth from before the LORD and consumed the burnt offering and the fat upon the altar; and when all the people saw it, they shouted, and fell on their faces" (v. 24).

Rejecting the Word (10:1-20)

Contrasting attitudes toward the commanding word of God are the focus of chapter 10. In one instance Nadab and Abihu were guilty of profaning the Lord's presence, while in another there are three illustrations of ways in which performing the Lord's word has priority. Throughout the chapter there is central concern for the sanctity of worship grounded in the holiness of God's presence. Profaning holy experiences is a constant temptation of ministry. Those who live daily in the midst of holy tasks may unconsciously develop callous attitudes. The challenge to be sensitive to the holiness of one's calling is intended for all believers. Figuratively, consuming fires still fall on the lives of those who abuse God's presence by profaning the holiness of ministry.

Profaning the Lord's presence (10:1-7).—To illustrate the hazard of ignoring the Lord's word concerning the sanctity of the altar, the sin of Nadab and Abihu, sons of Aaron, was used as an object lesson. The passage was linked to the previous chapter by the role that fire plays in each. In chapter 9 the Lord sent fire to consume the sacrifice. But chapter 10 tells of a consuming fire that destroyed Nadab and Abihu for placing "unholy fire" on the altar. They profaned the holiness not only of the altar but also of God's presence. We perceive the clear lines of the writer's purpose: No one, not even sons of Aaron, may profane the Lord's presence with impunity.

Performing the Lord's word (10:8-20).—In contrast to the rejection of the Lord's word typified in the sin of Nadab and Abihu, verses 8-20 illustrate three ways in which the sanctity of the altar is to be maintained.

First, the sanctity of the altar was protected by prohibiting wine and strong drink for priests. Since such prohibitions were not enjoined generally upon the people as a whole, why should they be for the priests? Probably the crux of the issue is the continuing rejection of leaven, and even fruit-honey, in the ritual practices of Israel (cf. Lev. 2:11). It was because of the fermentation process related to wine and strong drink that these were prohibited. Leaven that was neither holy nor clean (v. 10) was prohibited.

Second, specific regulations directed where communion-type sacrifices were to be eaten. For example, the cereal offering which had been offered on the altar was "most holy" and could be eaten by the priests only, and then only in a holy place (vv. 12-13). The breast that was waved during the peace offering (hence "wave offering," cf. Lev. 7:30-36) together with the thigh was given as a perpetual right of the priest and formed part of his compensation. This portion of the sacrifice could be eaten "in any clean place" (v. 14).

Third, the inappropriate treatment of the "goat of the sin offering" (v. 16) formed a third object lesson illustrating the sanctity of the altar. Apparently the goat offered as a second sin offering (9:15) was burned. Instead, the priests should have eaten the sin offering in the sanctuary since it was "most holy" (v. 17). For in eating the sin offering the priests in some manner were understood to have taken the sin of the people upon themselves. Unless the ministering priest shared the burden of the people, he could not bear that burden to God.

The Lord's Word for Dedicating National Life

11:1 to 15:33

The Lord's word for the dedication of life included not only sacrifice which made possible new qualities of relationship with the Lord (1:1 to 7:38), and the dedication of a ministry committed to intercession and atonement (8:1 to 10:20), but also the dedication of the whole nation through appropriate regard for the "clean" and the "unclean" (11:1 to 15:33). Using the phrase "the LORD said to Moses" as a recurring point of division within the narrative, we can isolate the following ways in which attitudes toward clean and unclean situations were the focus for the dedication of national life. These are: clean and unclean animals (11:1-47), the purification of women (12:1-8), tests for leprosy (13:1-59), cleansing of leprosy (14:1-32), purifying houses infected through leprosy or mildew (TEV; cf. 14:33-57), and bodily discharges (15:1-33). These emphases are grounded in four fundamental concerns: clean and unclean animals, purification of women, leprosy, and bodily discharges.

Categories of "clean" and "unclean" were ritual concerns directly related to the concept of the holy. God was holy, one completely other than all creation. Only those persons and nonhuman objects which were ritually clean could be related to him. Persons achieved this state largely through the sacrificial system, and they maintained this in large part by avoiding contact with the "unclean." Both the "clean" and the "unclean" were contagious, and one could contaminate the clean through contact with the unclean. That which belonged to another god was unclean in early Israel, and separate words were used for persons or objects holy to the God of Israel and to other gods. Mysterious areas of life often constituted the "unclean"; sexual intercourse, death, normal bodily wastes together with other bodily issues, childbirth, and diseases commonly identified as leprosy. Foreign-born persons or objects were also unclean and could not relate to the worship center unless appropriately cleansed through a prescribed ritual.

How is the present-day interpreter of Leviticus to understand these views? How do they convey a contemporary revelation of God's purpose? First, religious practices universally reflect external cultural patterns of the times, however much those cultural patterns became vehicles for divine truth. So Israel used the concepts of "unclean" and "clean" common to her culture. But in doing so she conveyed a depth of understanding of God and the necessity for mediation and cleansing which contemporary Christianity and Judaism still acknowledge.

Second, it may be of help to keep in focus an observation of Paul related to an altogether different context. "But we have this treasure in earthen vessels, to show that the transcendent power belongs to God and not to us" (2 Cor. 4:7). The attitude of Israel toward clean and unclean persons and nonhuman phenomena was an earthen vessel, which served as a vehicle to bear God's revelation. Conditioned by time and culture, the frailty of such a literary vehicle shows that "the transcendent power belongs to God." It is God through his Spirit who authenticates his message as one of authority for the believer. As we study we try to discover that treasure in an earthen vessel which speaks of clean and unclean animals, purification rites for women, the uncleanness of leprosy, and bodily discharges.

Distinguishing Between Clean and Unclean Animals (11:1-47)

Perhaps there was no single rationale for the identification of certain animals as unclean. But among those that have been suggested are, *first,* hygienic principles. One may legitimately argue that eating certain prohibited animals, especially in the climate of the ancient Near East, was precluded on the basis of sound hygiene.

Second, the religious veneration or use in sacrifice of these animals by non-Israelites was probably a primary cause for the "unclean" category in Israel. Although it is no longer possible to isolate which particular animals were so used in the rituals of other cultures, the fact that they are now taken up into the "clean" and "unclean" category lends weight to this alternative. For example, the pig was probably unclean for Israel because of its use in Canaanite sacrifice, as well as in Babylonia, Cyprus, and Syria.

It is also possible that the problem of unclean animals was influenced by some idea or practice no longer known. Such prohibitions had simply become "the command of God." Or one living then might have answered, "We just don't eat camel meat." Such a hypothetical response parallels the rationale given today for persons of British descent who largely refuse to eat horse meat. One scholar suggests that there was a clear religious principle operative in prior centuries. Heathen Saxons believed that such flesh was sacred to the god Odin; and when they became Christians, horse flesh was forbidden to avoid compromising the new faith with old religious practices. Also among non-Israelites prior to the time of Israel's existence, foods originally may have been avoided for hygienic reasons and placed in the category of the forbidden. Knowing of these "unclean" foods which were prohibited because of their "evil" effects (and every action was controlled by a deity, whether beneficient or malignant), Israel also rejected such food. But they did so for theological or religious reasons, not for hygienic reasons.

A *third* reason for rejecting some of the animals was grounded in the veneration of blood in the Old Testament and the manner in which life was thought to reside in the blood. Since life was uniquely of God, blood was always given back to God ritually, and no one could appropriate it. Carrion birds and animals that ate flesh were precluded for Israel, as were animals that "died of themselves," since the blood had not been dedicated appropriately to God.

But the most significant issue in regard to clean and unclean animals is: What theological understanding did Israel communicate through these practices? *First*, through them Israel affirmed her commitment to live a life dedicated solely to God and to make use only of those phenomena and objects appropriate to his presence. Even in the Christian era Paul was willing to accept the distinction between clean and unclean as it applied to meat which had been offered to idols (1 Cor. 8:1-13). Through the use of cultural practices characteristic of religious experience at a certain level of development, Paul bore witness to the uniqueness of God and especially to his purity. In like manner, although not having risen to see beyond the literal prohibition, ancient Israel bore testimony to the purity of God and his presence in their lives by following ceremonial laws which governed their food. *Second,* by so observing the ritual laws, Israel affirmed to the world that they belonged to Yahweh, the God of Israel. The distinctiveness of the dietary laws was a visible manifestation of the distinctiveness of Israel's faith. Such practices identified them as people of God. This is clearly stated as the fundamental rationale in the list of clean and unclean foods in Deuteronomy 14:1. Because Israel belonged to the Lord, they were to manifest that relationship in their observance of a specified life-style.

The laws themselves are self-evident in their intent, although some of the animals are unique to the Middle East, and some may be unknown today. It remains only to indicate the structure which the writer/compiler of the book used in collecting the dietary laws of chapter 11. First, there are lists of animals which may or may not be eaten, stipulations related to becoming unclean by touching certain animals, and the prohibition of eating any swarming thing. Then the writer/compiler also classified animals according to land, sea, and air. The closing explanatory note (11:46-47) is an especially helpful summary on the purpose of the chapter.

In the Introduction we noted that Leviticus is a book of practice, not of theory. Israel utilized cultural practices of their day and infused them with religious meaning. This quality of incarnational reality characterizes people of God in every cultural era. The Word must become flesh if it is to be appropriated (John 1:1-18). And it "becomes flesh," to use that New Testament expression, in the cultural forms of a given era in history. Using common attitudes of "clean" and "unclean," Israel manifested through culturally conditioned dietary laws their commitment to the uniqueness of God and to the reality of their relationship to him. They demonstrated to the world that they belonged to him by the way they lived. Theirs was a noble ideal, worthy of modern emulation.

Purifying Women Following Childbirth (12:1-8)

The same conditional nature which characterizes other purification laws applies to the Levitical statement on purifying women following childbirth. No one today should associate uncleanness with childbirth or affirm the inferior role of woman reflected in this chapter. But Israel acted in light of culture to bring all of life into the realm of God's presence. As suggested previously, "uncleanness" often came about in the face of great mystery. Unable to understand phenomena or assuming that such phenomena were related to malignant or evil powers, ancient Israel ascribed those to the "unclean." Procreation, including semen itself (Lev. 15:16) and childbirth (12:1 ff.) were linked with mystery. Blood associated with menstruation (15:19) or childbirth was "unclean" because such blood had not been ritually dedicated to God. Given Israel's understanding of "clean" and "unclean," the proper response to those mysterious acts was to require rituals of purification.

Uncleanness through childbirth (12:1-5).—When a male child was born, the mother was unclean for seven days, the same stipulation related to menstruation, and continued in her impurity for thirty-three days—giving a total period of forty days as the time of impurity following the birth of a male. The cultic inferiority of the female was revealed by doubling each of the periods of time related to uncleanness. With the same uncleanness associated with menstruation, a mother of a female was unclean for two weeks, not one week as in the case of a male child (v. 5). She continued to be unclean for sixty-six days, not thirty-three days—for a period of uncleanness totaling eighty days. Such uncleanness precluded sexual activity, and one might well argue that the physiological well-being of the mother prompted the ban. While physiological benefits did occur, this is a modern conception, hardly operative in the consciousness of Israel. But the taboo attendant to uncleanness, although religiously grounded, was physiologically beneficent.

Purification through sacrifice (12:6-8).—In a most unusual provision, the woman made her own sacrifice, offering a double sacrifice of burnt offering and sin offering. The offering required was modest, a lamb for a burnt offering and a turtle-dove or a young pigeon for a sin offering. If she could not afford this, a bird could be offered for the burnt offering and another for the sin offering.

So life was restored to its purity and to its acceptability before God. And so, also, did Israel manifest her fidelity to the uniqueness of God for the full range of life, however mysterious the elements of cause and effect related to the ritual of purification,

Purifying Regulations Concerning Leprosy (13:1 to 14:57)

The Bible never pronounces leprosy a sin, although with consistency it identifies persons with leprosy as "unclean." The priests were charged with diagnosing leprosy and determined healing or cleansing, as well as the purification of a leper's house.

Diagnosing leprosy (13:1-59).—The Hebrew term which is translated "leprosy" is generic and describes the manifestation of an eruptive skin disease. The equivalent Greek term identifies an ailment characterized by scaly patches on the skin and was used by a number of Greek writers. Harrison, in a succinct and excellent article on leprosy, suggests that the term was indefinite with the result that Greek translators of the Old Testament used it to characterize "psoriasis, leucodermia, ringworm, and the like, as well as true leprosy." [3] He further suggests that another Greek medical term, elephantiasis, or "elephantiasis Graecorum" described a much more serious disease, with symptoms like those of modern leprosy or Hansen's disease. Harrison convincingly proposes that in the Middle Ages, European medical writings used the Vulgate lepra as a designation of elephantiasis Graecorum so that symptoms of that much-feared disease were ascribed to all ailments associated with the generic Hebrew word. From this confusion arose the belief that the chronic, hopeless, medieval European leprosy was being described by the biblical references.

Following the widely varying instructions of chapter 13, if the priest discovered that the person had a skin disease of whatever sort, he was declared "unclean." Again, one might argue that isolation outside the community, as specified for lepers (v. 46), was a medical procedure designed to prevent contagious infection. Such isolation did have this effect. But the rationale grew out of religious considerations: The person was "unclean" and could no longer live in a community made "clean" through appropriate ritual. It was religious motivation and commitment which prompted the action, and the priest remained a religious leader of ritual, not the precursor of public health officials. Yet having said this, we acknowledge in this instance, as in others, that "good religion" often makes for "good health." But fundamentally, in identifying and isolating the leprous person, whatever the medical nature of the malady may have been, the intent of the action was to protect the dedicated nature of the community.

Cleansing leprosy (14:1-32).—Once leprosy had been healed, the leper presented himself to the priest for examination and purification. If the examination by the priest proved that he was indeed healed, then the person began a somewhat complicated process of purification. The first part of the ceremony suggests a process of transference.

Two birds were brought to the sanctuary. One was killed and the other, after being sprinkled with the blood of the former, was allowed to fly away into the field. Afterward, the worshiper washed his clothes and shaved his hair; then he was permitted to go into the camp. After going into the camp he could not enter his tent, however, but was required to dwell outside his tent for seven days. On the eighth day the sacrifices described in verses 10-21 were offered, and the person through that ritual was restored to a state of ceremonial "cleanness." Should he be a poor person and unable to afford the prescribed sacrifice (vv. 10-21), he could offer the alternative (vv. 21-32).

Purifying a house (14:33-53).—Since not only persons but nonhuman objects could be clean or unclean, the house of a leper was declared unclean. Some do assume, however, that the house was infected with mildew (TEV) and not with leprosy. Assuming that leprosy was involved, following the healing of the leper, the house had to be restored to its condition of cleanness. Specific details for this are described in three paragraphs. Old Testament Israel did not deal with secondary causes, and in early Israel all action ultimately was ascribed to God. So in this instance, in describing an outbreak of "leprosy," verse 34 reports the Lord saying, "I put a leprous disease in a house." The fuller revelation of God within Scripture and church acknowledges the contingencies of secondary sources as causal factors in historical events. But the biblical writer dealt only with that ultimate relationship, his relationship with God. It was this that must be restored, however that communion may have been destroyed.

Uncleanness Through Bodily Discharges (15:1-33)

We cannot assume that the physiology of the human body was as well known in ancient times as in the twentieth century. After all, it was not until the work of William Harvey in the seventeenth century that the functioning of the heart began to be fully understood. How mysterious the functioning of the human body was to ancient persons remains beyond conception. Especially were forces related to life, blood, sexual relations, and inexplicable discharges of the body sources of mystery. These mysterious areas of life were treated with utmost care to protect the ritually clean status of the community. Each problem required ritual cleansing. Not only was this so because of general areas of mystery associated with the phenomena, but also because in each instance the phenomenon related to the genital area. This factor alone would have required the utmost care in maintaining holiness or "cleanness." Here one deals with the origins of life and the full range of sexuality and its significance for the holy community (cf. Lev. 18:1-30).

Discharge from a male (15:1-12).—The ritual of purification prescribed for a male with a discharge is adequately clear, reflecting practices comparable to those previously described. The troubling issue here is the nature of the discharge, although one may rightly assume that it is either genital or rectal (v. 6). The malady itself involved a discharge which could remain on the bed or where the man sat. The text also suggests a continuing discharge as one feature of the ailment: "his body runs with his discharge" (v. 3). Since no one of these descriptions is definitive, the meaning of the word itself is the key to understanding the nature of the problem. The Hebrew word means an issue, always from the genitals of a man or woman. Since semen is considered elsewhere (vv. 16-18), this "issue" apparently involved another kind of emission.

An emission of semen (15:16-18).—Semen precipitated uncleanness for a man. Or "if a man lies with a woman," both were unclean and must bathe themselves in water, remaining unclean until the evening. Again, behind the taboo was the fundamental mystery associated with sexual activity, which in turn was grounded in the mystery of life.

Menstruation (15:19-24).—During her regular menstrual period a woman was unclean and remained impure for seven days afterward. Anyone touching her, as well as clothing or places where she might lie or sit, was unclean. No man could have intercourse with her within the seven-day period of time, or he too would be unclean for seven days. Common attitudes toward blood (cf. Lev. 17:1 ff.) and sexuality formed the background for this ritual provision.

Discharging blood (15:25-33).—The stipulations concerning a continuing vaginal discharge precipitated the same uncleanness as menstruation. Once the discharge ceased, appropriate sacrifices were offered to assure ritual purification. Note that no offering was required in the case of menstruation, probably because of the regularity of the period as opposed to the continuing discharge.

In each of these four instances, the gravity of the problem was compounded because the source of the discharge was in the genital area. The focus of concern was not only with the mystery of the phenomenon, its irregularity, its ill effects, or attitudes toward blood, but the sexual aspect of the discharge. Thus the phenomenon of human sexuality appeared in the ritual law as a concern of high priority for the people of God, however that priority manifested itself.

In assessing the laws of purification (11:1 to 15:33) attention has focused on the manner in which Israel used practices common to her time to manifest dedication to the Lord. Although far removed in practice from contemporary life, such laws remain a constant reminder to hallow one's relationships with God, to implement through contemporary understanding one's commitment to God, and to manifest by a deliberate life-style that we are in fact people of God at a particular juncture in the historical pilgrimage of God's people.

The Lord's Word for Atoning for Sin
16:1-34

This narrative of the ritual of atonement is probably more significant for the Christian than any other section in Leviticus. Not only was this a central focus in the faith of Israel; the essence of the ritual was interpreted by early Christians as having been fulfilled in the ministry of Jesus. Especially was his death on the cross interpreted in terms of an atonement. In contemporary Judaism Yom Kippur remains a central focus. And for all who commit their lives to the Lord, the theological foundations expressed through such a special day of atonement speak with full, rich tones of the forgiveness and the relationships which are ours because of God's atoning work. As is true in many of the chapters of instruction in Leviticus, this summary provides an excellent overview of purpose: "And this shall be . . . that atonement may be made for the people of Israel once in the year because of all their sins" (16:34). There were four basic steps in the ritual: (1) preparing the priest and forgiving the priestly minister, (2) sacrificing the sin offering for the people, (3) driving the goat into the wilderness, and (4) purifying those associated with the sacrificial rites.

The Preparation and Forgiveness of the Priestly Minister (16:1-6, 11-14)

The attention given to the preparation of Aaron and the forgiveness of his sin reaffirms the thesis that no minister can lead people where he has not been. No person can speak of the forgiveness of sins whose own sin has not been forgiven. A worship leader has no right of access to the holy place of worship whose sin remains unconfessed and thus unforgiven. The day of Atonement began with Aaron, not with the people.

Forgiving the Congregation (16:7-10,15-19)

Two goats were required in the ritual of atonement, one for the congregation and one for Azazel. The first was a normative sin offering for the people. The unique aspect of the sacrifice focused on the "holy of holies," known more commonly in the Old Testament as "the most holy place." The ritual of atonement itself was an uncommon practice in that it occurred on an annual cycle (v. 29) and Aaron did not normally go into the holy place (v. 2). Again, as in the case of the sacrifice for Aaron's sin (vv. 11-14), the blood was taken within the most holy place and sprinkled on the mercy seat and before it. Following the sprinkling of the most holy place, the priest did the same for the tent of meeting and the altar in the outer court. The necessity for this ritual emerges in the closing verse. Because of the accumulation of sin generated through the repeated offering of sacrifices during the year, the altar had to be purged on an annual basis (v. 19). It was, in effect, reconsecrated to its original state of holiness which characterized it at the time of its consecration during the ordination of the priests.

Sending Away Congregational Sin (16:7-10,20-22)

The ritual of atonement involved the selection of two goats, after which lots were cast to determine which was for the Lord and which was for Azazel. The first goat having been sacrificed (vv. 15-19), the priest then led in a ritual in which he laid both hands on the other goat's head, symbolically identifying corporate Israel with the sacrifice. Then he confessed over the sacrificial animal "all the iniquities of the people of Israel, and all their transgressions, all their sins" (v. 21). The goat was then driven into the wilderness by an attendant.

In this symbolic ritual the sacrificial animal "shall bear all their iniquities upon him to a solitary land."

The structure of the ritual is clear, as are the implications for the necessity of a mediator in the reality of forgiveness. Not only was there the necessity for a priestly person like Aaron, but the people needed a sacrifice to bear their sins "to a solitary land."

The fundamental issue related to the ritual focuses on the rather puzzling reference to Azazel. What is meant by that term and by the practice to which the name was related? The Hebrew word was probably derived from a word meaning "to remove." The word has been interpreted as a proper noun referring to a spirit that haunted the desert, or, in the case of some who see this as a late term related to Jewish angelology, to a fallen angel. When the Old Testament was translated into Greek, the translators used a word meaning "for sending away." The name remains enigmatic, and it is unlikely that one can appropriately be more specific. But the ceremony has marks of being an ancient one, and the reference to Azazel is probably to a specific demon or evil spirit of the desert, however difficult this may make the interpretation of sending the sin away to the demon. Originally, the text probably focused on appeasing such a symbolic figure of evil.

Purifying Ceremonial Leaders (16:23-28)

Reflecting the common view in ancient Israel which presupposed that evil was contagious, those persons primarily involved in the ritual of atonement participated in purification rites. This was true of Aaron as well as the attendant who led the goat into the wilderness.

Meeting a Continuing Need (16:29-34)

Because the people of God need to experience continuing forgiveness, the atonement ritual was prescribed as an annual ceremony. Dated in the seventh month, on the tenth day, the time of atonement came in early fall each year. Because sin is recapitulated in society, so the ritual of forgiveness is an everlasting statute. But for the Christian community it is a statute which found its fulfillment in Jesus Christ. Nowhere is this made clearer than in the book of Hebrews: "But when Christ appeared as a high priest . . . he entered once for all into the Holy Place, taking not the blood of goats and calves but his own blood, thus securing an eternal redemption" (Heb. 9:11-

12). That which was "an everlasting statute" in Leviticus (16:34) has been superseded by one who brought eternal redemption. In Jesus Christ believers discover one who bears their sin into a solitary land whence it never returns to haunt them as Azazel haunted the wastelands of the desert.

The Lord's Word for Dedicating Relationships
17:1 to 26:46

This section of Leviticus is commonly known as the "Holiness Code" and is the oldest collection of laws in the book, probably circulating as a separate collection. Late in the history of Israel's existence it was brought into the unified collection of ritual stipulations now found in Leviticus. As the name implies, the material is uniquely concerned with the holiness of God, which it seeks both to protect and to recreate in the relationships which Israel sustained in daily life and worship. Holiness affirms that the people of God uniquely belong to the Lord, who is himself wholly other than both human and nonhuman aspects of creation. It manifests itself in the quality of those relationships sustained by the people of God. Among the ways by which holiness may be reflected through relationships are: *life, sexuality, human behavior, covenant faithfulness, worship,* and *freedom.* In these six areas of relationship the dedication of the Lord's people may be manifest to one another, to those outside the covenant, and to God.

The Sanctity of Life (17:1-16)

Life is sacred because it belongs to God. More so, man himself is so made in the image of God that to shed the blood of another is to forfeit one's life (Gen. 9:6). For this reason the sixth commandment said, "You shall not kill" (Ex. 20:13). On that basis one also builds the interlocking structure of personal relationships: what we do to one another, we in some mysterious way do to God (cf. Matt. 25:40).

Life is the gift of God, lived out in stewardship and ultimately returned to him. Life is sacred, as is human personality, because it is uniquely related to God.

Where does life reside? For modern persons with a holistic view of personality and a reasonable understanding of physiology, a variety of answers might be given. But for the ancient Israelite the answer was simple: Life is in the blood (Lev. 17:14). Perhaps this conclusion rested on seeing an animal or a person bleed to death. Because life, sacred to God, was located in the blood, to blood also was given unusual sanctity. Blood could not be consumed in normative ways as food. Even in sacrificial rites the blood was returned to God by sprinkling or dashing it on the altar or other places in the sanctuary. Blood belonged to God because life belonged to him. Hence both were sacred.

Four stipulations uniquely governed Israel's relationship to blood. Any animal slain must be slaughtered at the sanctuary as a peace offering to God (vv. 1-7). No person could offer sacrifices at a place other than the sanctuary, as might have been done by the head of household in early times (vv. 8-9). No person was permitted to eat blood (vv. 10-13), and nothing which "dies of itself" (v. 15), whatever the manner of death, could be eaten (vv. 14-16). Through those regulations Israel sanctified the blood, recognizing that it, like God, was "wholly other" than the human or animal order.

Reverence for life rests at the core of these regulations, for it was not merely blood but life which was of fundamental concern. Recognizing the sanctity of all life (blood) was another way by which people of the covenant manifested dedication to God. So fidelity and dedication to God continue, even to this day, to manifest themselves through reverence for life. Respect for human personality and the dignity accorded persons made in the image of God are ways in which contemporary believers continue to express their dedication to the Lord.

The Sanctity of Sexuality (18:1-30)

Whatever the sexual standards of other cultures (18:3), Israel manifested dedication to God through appropriate sexual conduct. Although the stipulations of chapter 18 focus on sexual aberrations and are in the form of prohibitions, they reflect the wholesome and positive assumption that human sexuality manifested through intercourse is an experience whose sanctity is to be protected. Because of the mysteries of sexual activity, the procreation of life, and the relationship of all life to God, sexual activity was sacred.

Sexual aberration: incest (vv. 6-18).—Technically, incest is defined by Webster as the crime of cohabitation between persons related within the degrees wherein marriage is prohibited by law. Using the word "nakedness" as a euphemism for cohabitation, Leviticus condemns nine incestuous relationships. Following the enunciation of a governing principle (v. 6), sexual relations were precluded with one's father or mother, stepmother, sister, whether full or half, granddaughter, cousin, aunt, daughter-in-law, and sister-in-law. Further, sexual relations were considered incestuous if they were with both a woman and her daughter (v. 17), or if one married two sisters (v. 18).

Sexual aberration: adultery (v. 20).—Following the prohibition of sexual activity during the time a woman was unclean because of her menstrual period (v. 19), sexual intercourse was excluded with a neighbor's wife.

Sexual aberration: child abuse (v. 21).—To "devote" a child by fire to Molech involved human sacrifice and was a crime discussed later in 20:2-5. But the inclusion of the practice in the larger context of sexual aberrations suggests that offering a child to Molech was also associated with sexual abuse. Although fundamentally repulsive to human sensibility, the problem is not unrelated to the contemporary exploitation of children for pornographic and sexual abuses.

Sexual aberration: homosexuality (v. 22).—Biblical religion presupposed heterosexual relationships as normative within the community of faith, despite the fact that cultures contemporary with both Old Testament and the New Testament times permitted homosexuality. The biblical injunction is clear: "You shall not lie with a male as with a woman."

Sexual aberration: bestiality (v. 23).—It was a perversion in Israel to practice bestiality.

The explicit, authoritative nature of the prohibitions are unique. First, they are phrased in the same style as the Ten Commandments and reflect the use of apodictic law, the "thou shalt not . . ." as opposed to the casuistic "If . . ." or "When . . ." This type of law is the direct, unconditioned command of God. Second, there is no ritual of forgiveness as with ritual infractions outside the Holiness Code (cf. 15:19-

30). Instead of a sacrifice of forgiveness, one "shall be cut off from among their people" (18:29). Exclusion from the community of Israel was the penalty for sexual aberrations. Actually, the phrase more likely refers to death than to banishment from the community.

The absolute seriousness with which the biblical community approached human sexuality stands in marked contrast to the casual attitude of contemporary society. More positively stated, the biblical narrative calls the church as heir both to the promises and to the responsibilities of ancient Israel to address sexuality as an effective means of manifesting dedication.

The Sanctity of Human Behavior (19:1-37)

The centrality of this chapter for human behavior is partially reflected in Jesus' use of part of it in formulating the great commandment: "But you shall love your neighbor as yourself" (v. 18; cf. Matt. 22:39; 5:43; 19:19). Such exhortation to appropriate human behavior is grounded in one's relationship to God: "You shall be holy; for I the LORD your God am holy" (v. 2). The root meaning of "holy" is to be set apart. For Israel, or for contemporary believers, to be holy has the fundamental meaning of belonging to God. Quite early in both Babylonia and in Israel, a temple prostitute was known as a "holy one," in the sense that the person served the deity. But when the concept of holiness was associated with the Lord, who was ethical and moral, the word came to have ethical connotations, especially by the eighth century B.C. So in this instance, to be holy as God is holy has ethical implications. If one uniquely belongs to the Lord, one will manifest the quality of that relationship through his behavior.

Although each behavioral category cannot be examined in detail, consider the wide ranges of human behavior which flow out of one's relationship with God: honoring parents (v. 3); leaving part of a field for the poor and the sojourner (vv. 9-10); refusing to steal, to deal falsely, or to lie (vv. 11-12); equity toward hired persons, as toward one's neighbors (vv. 13-14); practicing justice (vv. 15-16), loving other persons (vv. 17-18); sexual restraint (vv. 20-22); refusing to make one's daughter a prostitute (vv. 29-30); honoring one's elders (v. 32); consideration for strangers (vv. 33-34); and honesty in business practices (vv. 35-37).

To these were added also faithfulness toward the Lord by revering the sabbath and maintaining fidelity to the Lord of revelation (vv.

3,30); sacrificing appropriately (vv. 5-8); observing ritual prescriptions for cattle breeding and horticulture (vv. 19,23-25); and fidelity to ritual practices (vv. 26-28). Such positive aspects of human behavior grew out of the relationship that Israel maintained with the Lord: "You shall be holy; for I the LORD your God am holy" (v. 2). So in every generation, believers manifest the quality of their dedication by the quality of their behavior.

The Sanctity of Covenant Fidelity (20:1-27)

Chapter 20 addresses essentially the same issues as chapter 18. The former chapter deals with prohibitions without immediate reference to punishment, while the latter chapter regards the infringements from the perspective of the death penalty. The two chapters appear to be independent of one another, despite the close similarity in subject matter. Chapter 20 does have a prefatory statement on covenant fidelity (vv. 1-9). Otherwise the emphases are essentially the same.

Commitment to covenant faith (vv. 1-9).—Verses 7-8 may constitute the original opening of the address; if so, the chapter began with the presupposition that the people of Israel were to consecrate themselves and be holy. Such foundation for the address is comparable to the holiness emphasis of 19:2 "You shall be holy; for I the LORD your God am holy." Conduct grows out of one's relationship with the Lord of covenant life.

Both the rejection of Molech worship (vv. 1-5) and the repudiation of false sources of revelation (v. 6) are consistent with the claim of God to religious and theological priority in the life of Israel, as suggested in the first commandment (cf. Ex. 20:3). "Mediums and wizards" (v. 6) may refer to the spirits of the dead. One might compare 1 Samuel 28:3 ff. for an illustration of this practice, which had previously been condemned in Leviticus. 19:31. Again, unless one's relationships with the Lord are proper, reflecting covenant fidelity, there are no adequate foundations for behavior indicative of the sanctity of one's life (cf. v. 7).

Consequences of sexual aberrations (vv. 10-21).—Sexual aberrations such as adultery, incest, homosexuality, and bestiality are consistently subject to death penalties, in one instance by burning (v. 14).

Clean and unclean decisions (vv. 22-27).—Because the Lord separated Israel from other people they too were to make distinctions between the clean and the unclean. The fundamental rationale for this distinction, together with the conduct specified in this and preceding chapters, is reflected in the sentence that becomes a recurring pattern and closes this chapter: "You shall be holy to me; for I the LORD am holy, and have separated you from the peoples, that you should be mine."

Although few would insist on the death penalty for the aberrations in conduct described in these chapters, and none rightly so, the severity of such penalties underscores the seriousness with which biblical Israel sought to maintain purity of conduct. Such seriousness is a constant reminder to every believer of God's claim for fidelity to covenant relationships assumed in committing oneself to the Lord. Such fidelity is a sacred responsibility, which grows out of one's relationship with the Lord.

The Sanctity of Worship (21:1 to 24:23)

Holiness was especially manifested through worship in all its varied forms. The Holiness Code (Lev. 17—26) is a collection of stipulations related to the holiness of life which developed independently of those sources uniquely related to the Jerusalem priests, as in the case of the remainder of Leviticus and most of Exodus 25—40. It is also independent of understandings of God's relationship with Israel which prevailed in the Northern and Southern Kingdoms. Because of this, much of the material found in 21:1 to 24:23 is supplementary to previous stipulations in Exodus and Leviticus. The primary concerns in protecting the sanctity of worship were the holiness of the priesthood (21:1-24), the sanctity of dedicated objects (22:1-33), a reverence for holy days (23:1-44), and the sanctity of ritual (24:1-23). Although contemporary persons are under no obligation to manifest holiness and the sanctity of worship through the same practices as pertained to Israel, the continuing exhortation to the holiness of worship and the sanctity of all related thereto is a word which must be heard if fidelity to the Lord is maintained.

The holiness of the priest (21:1-24).—As suggested previously, a fundamental question for those who worship God concerns the way in which God, who is wholly other than human and nonhuman creation, can be approached. Simply stated, this question was resolved through the principle of mediation. As Job longed for an umpire who might lay his hand upon both him and God (Job 9:33), so all need a mediator—one with access to God but who stands among persons.

For Old Testament faith the priest fulfilled this function, and it was
required that the holiness of his life be maintained constantly.

In summary fashion, the priest maintained holiness through refusing
either to participate in funeral ceremonies (vv. 1-6,10-12) or to marry
a woman who had been a prostitute, who was not a virgin, or who
had been divorced (vv. 7-9,13-15). Holiness was also assured by select-
ing priests from among men without physical defects (vv. 16-24). Each
of these involved "unclean" categories: association with a dead body,
sexual relations prior to marriage, and physical defects.

The sanctity of dedicated offerings (22:1-33).—All offerings dedicated to the Lord were uniquely holy and consequently were protected from "unclean" persons. Priests were warned at the threat
of death not to profane the Lord when they were unclean, whether
through leprosy or death or unclean animals. "Outsiders" also were
prohibited from association with holy things, although a slave could
be accepted. Offerings which were brought to the Lord were sanctified
through an appropriate ritual of sacrifice. One could not merely present one's gift to the Lord, not even the freewill offering (v. 18).
Additionally, specific proscriptions pertained to the sacrificial animal:
the number of days it remained with its mother, prohibition against
killing it and its mother on the same day (v. 28), and regulations for
eating the sacrifice (v. 30).

Attention has been given to these details, which are so far removed
from contemporary society, with no view to encouraging their literal
implementation. They are cited as evidence of the degree of seriousness with which Israel maintained the holiness of dedicated offerings.
Foundational to those practices was an appreciation for the mystery
and majesty of God which contemporary society has abandoned—
on occasion, even in worship.

Reverence for holy days (23:1-44).—Through the dedication of a
day such as the sabbath, or festal days related to other religious celebrations, Israel symbolically dedicated all of time to the Lord. Also, in
ceremonies celebrating the Exodus event and the wilderness experience, Israel affirmed the historical nature of their religious experience.
More so, the past event lived again for the worshiping community;
and contemporary persons were able, with relevance for their own
times, to participate in the saving acts of God. In addition to the
sabbath (vv. 1-4), Israel recognized five festivals: Passover and Unleavened Bread during March to April (vv. 5-14); Harvest Festival, or

Pentecost, coming fifty days after Passover/Unleavened Bread during
May to June (vv. 15-22); the New Year Festival, or Feast of Trumpets,
which came to early fall during September to October (vv. 23-25);
the day of Atonement during September to October (vv. 26-32); and
the Festival of Shelters or Booths during September to October, re-
minding Israel of the time of wandering (vv. 33-34).

Passover was originally a spring festival associated with the time
of lambing, to which the feast of unleavened bread was joined in
celebrating the deliverance from Egypt. Pentecost, sometimes called
the Feast of Weeks, was a one-day ceremony which celebrated the
end of the grain harvest (initiated with the offering of the sheaf of
barley during the Feast of Unleavened Bread) and the beginning of
the fruit harvest. The Feast of Tabernacles or Booths was kept for
seven days, beginning on the fifteenth day of the seventh month,
and combined the celebration of the grape harvest and the wandering
in the wilderness. Israel's celebrations combined the goodness of God
manifested through the agricultural year with his grace in acts of
historical deliverance. In so doing she bore witness to her dedication
of all life to the Lord.

The sanctity of ritual (24:1-23).—Concern for both ritual and ethical
conduct are combined in fitting fashion within this chapter, suggesting
the propriety of both. For Israel affirmed the appropriate role of ritual
(vv. 1-9) while maintaining ethical stipulations much like those of
the Ten Commandments and the laws in the book of the Covenant
(Ex. 21—24). In the first instance, specific instructions were given
concerning attention to the lights in the sanctuary. The lampstand
within the tabernacle (later the Temple) fulfilled more than the functional purpose of lighting an otherwise dark room. Although created
for aesthetic reasons, its primary purpose was to symbolize the presence of God as light. Indeed, it drew together the role of light in
the context of darkness, which characterized religion prior to the
creation of Israel as a nation. The bread also was given as a perpetual
commandment, and the presence of the bread not only reminded
Israel of the manna given in the wilderness, but more significantly
testified to Israel's continuing dependence upon the Lord for suste-
nance.

Ethical concern in the context of holiness was emphasized through
the story of the Egyptian, married to an Israelite woman, who cursed
the Lord and was stoned to death. This led to the stipulation that

any person cursing God should suffer a similar fate (vv. 10-16). But to this there also were added stipulations concerning murder, the destruction of an animal belonging to another person, and injury to a person. Not only was there a prescribed ritual for pleasing the Lord; there was also a prescribed pattern of ethical conduct.

The Sanctity of Freedom: Land and Persons (25:1-55)

The sanctity of both land and persons was affirmed in the laws of release. For in releasing the land and persons according to a calendar cycle, Israel recognized that both belonged to God. In the finest sense, both the earth and persons were holy in that they belonged to the Lord. Man was a steward of the land, and within the cultural patterns of the ancient world he was also a steward of persons. Through their relationship to the land and to other persons, Israel affirmed their dedication to the Lord. For modern persons living in an era when the earth is ravished without regard to such stewardship, Israel's ancient understanding of the sanctity of the land is an appropriate foundation block for a theology of ecology. The same is true of persons; if all persons belong to the Lord, and if we acknowledge this in our relationships with them as Israel did in the laws of freedom, then there emerges a foundation stone for a theology of interpersonal relationships as well as corporate concern for persons of need.

Freedom for land and persons came during the so-called sabbatical year, which came every seventh year (vv. 1-7,18-22). It also occurred during the fiftieth year, following the analogy of seven seven-year periods. No fields were to be planted during the sabbatical year (v. 4), just as no labor was done on the sabbath day. In both instances Israel testified through these symbols that time and land belong to God, and by letting it return to its primal condition as at creation they affirmed that reality. During the fiftieth year property reverted to the original owner (v. 10); fields lay fallow as in the sabbatical year (v. 11); and persons who because of poverty had sold themselves as slaves (vv. 39-46) were set free, with the proviso that if slaves were needed they should be bought "from the nations that are round about you" (v. 44).

Inherent in these laws and others in the chapter is the thesis that man is the steward of creation. Nothing belongs to him in the ultimate sense; everything belongs to God. This operative principle was intended to transform attitudes toward land and persons. Freedom was sacred and holy because of its relationship to the Lord. All of creation is the Lord's, and to set creation free is to acknowledge that sanctity. So God's continuing call is: Free the land, free the poor, free all who are encumbered. Freedom acknowledges that all creation is sacred, belonging not to persons but to the Lord.

Sanctity Through Choices (26:1-46)

Sanctity comes through choices, and the closing chapter of the Holiness Code (17—26) sets before Israel the blessings of obedience and the punishments of disobedience. The prerequisite nature of holiness as a relationship required to experience the presence of God was reaffirmed. Yet the choice remained that of persons. Individuals and corporate entities may obey or disobey.

Blessings of obedience (26:1-13).—For those who live with qualities of commitment described in chapters 17—26, there is the promise of rain in its season and the increase of the land (vv. 4-5). Peace shall come to those who honor God, and none need be afraid. The Lord will "have regard" for them and bounteously provide for their needs. Most significantly, he will "walk among" them, and they will belong to each other. The basis for that confident hope is found in verse 13.

The punishments of disobedience (26:14).—Life apart from God brought the terror of life, consumption and fever, and defeat by one's enemies, together with the destruction of the pride of power (vv. 14-20). If people would not learn from the discipline of history, then further disasters would follow. Ultimately the Lord himself would oppose them. In a passage which reflects the perspective of the postexilic period, the writer/compiler concluded by referring to the horror of seige and warfare (vv. 27-34) and to the desolation of those who "pine away in your enemies' land" (v. 39). But even from the enemy's land, if people "confess their iniquity," there was hope for the future. God would remember the covenant and bring the people back to the devastated land (vv. 40-45).

In all of this, one confronts a theological interpretation of history. Israel believed that God was the god of history and that history was the history of God. Such a theocentric view of history gave meaning to individual lives and purpose to nations. It is to the difficult challenge

of identifying the shadowed form of God behind the turbulent events
of history that the people of God in every age are called. God is
there, often unseen, but present in his providence. The choice to
acknowledge him was theirs, as it is ours. Holiness is a choice that
must be exercised, a yes or a no that must be given to God.

The Lord's Word for Dedicating
Possessions
27:1-34

Commentators generally assume that chapter 27 is an appendix
on vows and tithes which has been added to the book, whether by
the original writer/compiler or later. That it is a separate address
may be substantiated by noting the thirty-sixth use of "The LORD
said to Moses" which appears in Leviticus (v. 1). But the primary
issue is the thesis that dedication to the Lord may be demonstrated
through vows and tithes. Through vows and tithes life may be transmitted to God.

The primary issue related to vows (vv. 1-29) concerned property
which was given to the Lord and in turn passed to the priests. For
whatever reason, whether personal need or a change of intent, a
person might reclaim that property upon the payment of a fee. But
the vow once made could not be revoked apart from restitution. In
making vows to the Lord, persons entered into commitments which
bound them irrevocably.

The stipulation concerning the tithe reflects a situation comparable
to the vow. Acknowledging the binding nature of the tithe, that one-
tenth of all belonged to the Lord, ritual law provided for reclaiming
the tithe. Since the tithe was paid in kind, whether grain, produce,
or however, this passed to the priests. If one wanted to "redeem
any of his tithe, he shall add a fifth to it" (v. 31). In this manner
both the worshiper and the priest achieved advantages. Worshipers
might on occasion prefer to have the produce; and at a time when
money had developed, the priest might find it advantageous to receive

the value of the offering in coins. Although related to vows and not tithes, it may be instructive to note the valuation in money specified for persons (vv. 1-7) and the valuation in shekels of grain (v. 16). "Shekels" probably refers to coins rather than to a unit of weight, suggesting that the narrative originated after the development of coins, hence in the postexilic period of time.

Notes

1. Ronald E. Clements, *The Broadman Bible Commentary* 3 (Nashville: Broadman Press, 1973), p. 13.

2. R. K. Harrison, *The Interpreter's Bible Dictionary,* Vol. K-Q (Nashville: Abingdon Press, 1962), p. 112.

NUMBERS

Introduction

The book of Numbers describes Israel's experience with the Lord in the wilderness. As such it is a study of God's providence in the life of an emerging nation. Too often Numbers is valued for little more than its lists of places, events, and persons. But the book is also a documentary on the way in which the Lord led the Hebrews for an entire generation before fulfilling their dreams of a land with a settled people. Just as the entire camp was established around the presence of God as symbolized in the tabernacle (chap. 2), so the whole book revolves around the centrality of God. Understanding the *name, contents, structure, purpose,* and *abiding truth* of the book may enhance its continuing value for the people of God.

The fourth book of the Bible takes its English name from that in the Latin Vulgate, *Numeri,* which was dependent on the Greek translation of the Old Testament. The name arose because of the numbering of the people, although it tells of only two censuses. Actually, the census is a relatively minor emphasis, and the name "Numbers" hardly comprehends the primary thrust of the book's contents. The name of the book in the Hebrew canon is "in the wilderness," which summarizes well the focus of the book. It is concerned with God's providence as he led the Hebrews through the wilderness following the Exodus out of Egypt and the sojourn at Mount Sinai.

Contents

Numbers is a combination of lists of persons and places associated with the migration of the Hebrews, and collections of stipulations that characterized Israel at varying times. It also tells of the migration itself, but those narratives do not show up until chapter 10. For this reason the reader may conclude that the book has little worth apart from providing one with lists. Yet when we seek to understand why the writer/compiler used particular material at a certain place, we discover the theological method of the writer to help our own understanding of the nature of God's providence. For example, one may read 1:1 to 10:10 and see only the census list, with regulations about temple servants, laws governing religious practice, offerings of leaders, and references to the tabernacle. But in this commentary the exposition of those chapters focuses on the centrality of the God to whom Israel belongs. Viewed as a series of concentric circles, the section is concerned with the fact that Israel belongs to God, as reflected in the census (chap. 1); God is the center of Israel's life (chap. 2); there is a shared ministry (chaps. 3—6); and persons respond appropriately to God's presence (7:1 to 10:10). Israel's migration was thus firmly planted in the presence of God and his centrality for the people. Like the beating of the human heart, their movement in history was distinguished by the palpitation of a divine purpose that infused history with the providence of God.

Purpose

What is the purpose of the book of Numbers? It is a study in the providence of God as he fulfills the promise made to the fathers that Israel should be both a land and a people (Gen. 12:1-3). We discover in Numbers the consistent focus on promise and fulfillment which runs throughout the first six books of the Bible. What God promises, God will fulfill, as he did in the conquest. This purpose is achieved by tracing the migration of Israel, including stipulations and narratives which described the movement of the people through the stages of Sinai, Kadesh, and Moab. Numbers shows that God is the God of history, and history is the history of God.

Abiding Truths

First, the book affirms *the reality of divine providence,* however hidden it may be by crisis and discouragement. The life of faith is bound up with a purpose whose dimensions transcend the limiting experiences of life. People of God are a pilgrim people, always on the way and never arriving in the absolute sense. God always stands before us, whether in wilderness or settled lands, to lead us in his will. Even in the wilderness, that land so isolated from deity in primitive thought, God led his people.

Second, *the centrality of God* is a central focus of the experiences at Sinai and beyond. This is especially emphasized in chapter 2, where the structure for the camp is described with the tabernacle at the center. Is there any other place for God than at the center of life, whether for ancient or modern persons?

The Centrality of God's Presence
1:1 to 10:10

That section of Scripture beginning at Exodus 19:1 and concluding with Numbers 10:10 is commonly known as the "Sinai Narrative." All the material within that large segment of the Old Testament is set in the region of Sinai. There God spoke from the mountain, and Israel responded on the plains below in a variety of ways—sometimes faithlessly, but on other occasions with vibrant, exemplary faith. In 1:1 to 10:10 one confronts the people of God preparing to move on from Sinai, bound up in the providence of God, as the promises made so long before to Abraham continued toward their fulfillment. Four central emphases characterize those preparations: the identification of God's people (1:1-54), the centrality of the divine presence symbolized by the position of the tabernacle (2:1-34), the servants of the sanctuary (3:1 to 6:27), and responding to the Lord's presence (7:1 to 10:10). But throughout each of these subsidiary themes there runs the centrality of God's presence as the integrating force in the experiences of God's people.

The First Census of God's People (1:1-54)

There are two censuses described in Numbers, one at Sinai (chap. 1) and the other on the plains of Moab, at the conclusion of the wilderness pilgrimage and prior to entering the land (chap. 26). A third census recorded in the Old Testament came near the end of David's reign when he commanded Joab to number the people (cf. 2 Sam. 24:2-9). To this, one might also add the numbering of the priests during the exile period (Ex. 22:1 ff.). That the census was not well regarded in later Israel is suggested by the manner in which the Chronicler ascribed its inception to Satan (cf. 1 Chron. 21:10), despite the earlier reason given for the census (cf. 2 Sam. 24:1).

Three objectives motivated taking a census in the Bible: taxation, manpower for war, and allotting the work of Levites in cultic service. The apparent purpose of the census in chapter 1 and again in chapter 26 was to establish the numerical strength of Israel's military force.

Yet there may well have been factors operative in the census other than the identification and enumeration of Israel's military forces.

For example, one recalls the manner in which the priestly writers consistently categorized and developed the whole of Israel's life according to patterns and groups. Whether one is dealing with creation, the attention given to genealogies, or the minute details given to the specifications for the worship center, this unique fascination with order and appropriate divisions suggests a rationale with theological grounds.

Also, the census itself was a prerogative reserved for God, and he alone keeps the register of those who are to live or die (cf. Ex. 32:32-33). David's census was condemned apparently because it abandoned the principles of holy war for a conscripted army.

Although there is no hard evidence, the similarity between the naming of the animals as a symbol of authority (Gen. 2:18-19) and the numbering of the people is so marked as to suggest lines of common theological significance. It is probable that there were psychological and theological connotations of counting and numbering which are lost to our era. But may it not be that numbering the people was a way of affirming that they belonged to God? Through this technique there was the affirmation of their identity as people of God. They were counted, singled out as belonging to God. The operative principle was cultic, not solely military, for by this act they were symbolically affirmed as "people of God" set on a holy war.

Leadership for the census (1:1-16).—From each of the twelve tribes a leader, "head of the house of his fathers," assisted in the census. Those included were twenty years old and up, male members of the community. The purpose of the census is stated in verse 3.

Numbering the people (1:17-46).—The people were registered by families, and within that category by "fathers' houses." The census appears to have been initiated about one month before departing from Sinai (cf. 1:1; 10:11). The text indicates the number of persons to have been 603,550, implying a population of approximately two million persons, since those in the census included only persons who were male and twenty years of age and upward. Some have suggested that such a large number was more appropriate to the census during the time of David than to the wilderness period. Others have seen in the double meaning of the Hebrew word for "thousand" the possibility that the writer intended not thousand but clan, which is another meaning of the word. Further, Hebrew letters were used in lieu of numbers such as arabic numerals in North America and elsewhere;

and it is interesting that the numerical equivalent for "sons of Israel" in Hebrew is 603 and possibly related to the 603,000. It remains intriguing, however, to see in the numbering of Israel a cultic act which identified Israel as the people of God.

Exemption from the census (1:47-54).—Because the Levites were charged with responsibility for the tabernacle, they were exempt from the census (v. 49). Thus, they were not liable to military service as were other male members of the community. Also, following the thesis that numbering uniquely identified persons with God, they were already uniquely the Lord's. Later in Numbers, for example, the Levites were given to God in lieu of the dedication or sacrifice of the firstborn (cf. 3:40-51).

The Centrality of Divine Presence: The Arrangement of the Camp (2:1-34)

The key to the significance of this chapter is in the location of the tabernacle in the center of the camp and the stipulation that it was to remain in the center of the tribes while on the line of march. Since the Lord was understood to dwell symbolically above the ark between the cherubim, it was actually the Lord's presence in the midst of his people which constituted the primary emphasis of the biblical writer.

The eastward encampment (2:1-9).—Given the priority of the east in ancient Israel, one would anticipate that the tribes which later came to prominence in Israel were identified with the eastward encampment. Judah (vv. 3-4), Issachar (vv. 5-6), and Zebulun (vv. 7-8) comprised the triad to the east of the tent of meeting.

The southern encampment (2:10-16).—Reuben, Simeon, and Gad constituted the tribes on the south, suggesting the lesser significance they occupied in later times, but the corresponding priority which they had over tribes to the west and to the north.

The westward encampment (2:18-24).—To the west of the tent of meeting were the tribes of Ephraim (v. 18), Manasseh (v. 20), and Benjamin (v. 22).

The northern encampment (2:25-31).—North of the tent of meeting were the following: Dan (v. 25), Asher (v. 27), and Naphtali (v. 29).

In addition to these four quadrants of the encampment, the tribe of Levi (although not counted in the census) encircled the tent of

meeting in the midst of the complex, thus guarding the holiness of
God against any encroachment.

Modern readers who do take time to read this chapter may carelessly
dismiss it as of no consequence. But two factors are uniquely significant. *First,* God dwells in the midst of his people, and they journey
with the Lord in their midst. Whether they were encamped or on
the march, the arrangement was the same. God was to be at the
center of life. *Second,* Numbers is as concerned in its own way as
was the book of Leviticus with protecting the holiness of God. That
quality of reverential awe and wonder in the presence of God's power
and mystery is such as to create moments when each person is aware
of the reality of the God who is beyond our being. This narrative
structured for ancient Israel an avenue whereby such an understanding of God might prevail. Those who lose such experiences of God's
holiness—of reverential awe and wonder in the presence of his power
and mystery—are liable in the process to lose the presence of God.
The two are inseparable, and it is more than mere coincidence that
the presence of God and the holiness of God are bound together in
the single concern of the biblical writer of chapter 2.

Servants of the Sanctuary (3:1 to 6:27)

Like concentric rings of a series of circles, the concerns of the book
of Numbers fall one inside the other: the affirmation through numbering the people that they are people of God (chap. 1), the centrality
of God within the midst of his people (chap. 2), and in chapter 3
the focus on those who serve the Lord within the sanctuary. The
history of the Levites is a complex issue that cannot be pursued at
this juncture. But it should be noted that in Israel the term "Levite"
may have indicated not only a tribal relationship but a professional
category. In either case, the Levites were the servants of the sanctuary,
distinguished from the priests who were commonly referred to as
Aaron's sons. As Levitical responsibilities were delineated in chapters
3 and 4, it is obvious that these two groups maintained a shared ministry, in which the Levites were especially charged with the responsibility of the tabernacle, and through which both priest and Levite sought
to maintain a holy community.

Sharing a ministry (3:1-51).—The priestly heritage is clearly delineated in verses 1-4, in which the "sons of Aaron" are equated with

"the anointed priests, whom he ordained to minister in the priest's office." It is apparent that the writer intends to comment on more than Nadab and Abihu, who forfeited the priesthood, and Eleazar and Ithamar, who faithfully "served as priests in the lifetime of Aaron their father." In discussing these two sons the writer treats them as prototypes of all priests who later were to serve in Israel. For an assessment of the priority of their role and the nature of their function in Israel, examine the book of Leviticus, especially chapters 1 through 10.

Primary in the writer's concern are the priestly assistants, the Levites, who fulfilled a shared ministry with the priests. It is to those ministers of the sanctuary, Gershon, Kohath, and Merari, that verses 5-39 give attention. From the earliest period of Israel's history, priests were not exclusively Levitical, although Levites were preferred (cf. Judg. 17:7-13) and later were the exclusive occupants of the priestly office. But the Levites as a category distinct from the priests should be seen as other than traditional priestly figures. They were essentially assistants to the priests, performing various necessary tasks at the local sanctuary and later at Jerusalem.

The three sons of Levi, Gershon, Kohath, and Merari, were forerunners of the Levites as priests' assistants in the same way that the sons of Aaron, Eleazar and Ithamar, were understood to have been the forerunners of the priests. Although the specific responsibilities of Levites were broader than transporting the tabernacle (cf. vv. 7-10), it was to the clans of Gershon, Kohath, and Merari that the transportation of the tabernacle was committed. The sons of Kohath had the most solemn responsibility, that of transporting "the ark, the table, the lampstand, the altars, the vessels of the sanctuary" (v. 31). While the other clans were provided beasts of burden and carts to help them, the sons of Kohath carried the sacred vessels upon their shoulders (7:1-11). The sons of Gershon were charged with the coverings for the tabernacle, the hangings, screens, etc. (vv. 22-26), and the sons of Merari were responsible for the frames of the tabernacle, the pillars, bases, etc. (vv. 33-39). If this strikes the modern reader as meaningless, one might well remember that the most common task can be transformed into a noble responsibility if one carries to the task an appropriate commitment to fulfill one's role. These were common tasks; yet even they have their place within the shared ministry of those who serve the sanctuary.

The chapter closes with an emphasis on the unique relationship of the Levites to the Lord. Every firstborn, human and animal, belonged to God. A firstborn animal might be sacrificed, but Israel had rejected the practice of sacrificing the firstborn person. Still, the firstborn did belong to God. In order to resolve this issue, verses 40-51 propose that the Levites and the firstborn of their cattle shall uniquely belong to the Lord rather than all firstborn persons. Although the chapter does reject child sacrifice, this is not the primary thrust of the narrative. For the writer's principal concern is to say that there is a unique relationship between the Levites and the Lord, one that can be explained in terms of the substitution of the Levite for the firstborn person. So theirs was a unique relationship that the tedium of common tasks could not erode. The joy of their service grew out of the nature of their relationship with God, not the level at which some might rate the importance of what they did.

Contemporary persons need to recapture the emphasis on the shared ministry that undergirds this chapter. There is a continuing need to discover in the dynamic quality of one's relationship with the Lord the validation of one's vocation.

Fulfilling a responsibility (4:1-49).—Essentially, chapter 4 is a more detailed expansion of the responsibilities of Gershon, Kohath, and Merari. The nature of those responsibilities are self-evident as one reads verses 1-33, and the census described in verses 34-49 is of the same order as the general census previously described in the first chapter. Examining the subsidiary responsibilities assigned to the Levites, one is impressed again with what might be called the "ministry of the commonplace." Many in the congregation of God anticipate meeting him in some unusual experiences. But the world still needs persons committed to a shared ministry of the common-place, persons able to discover that no task fulfilled as an expression of one's faith should be despised. For God has the strangest way of turning our commonplace events into holy events as he fills them with his presence.

Maintaining a holy community (5:1 to 6:27).—Already, the book of Leviticus has preserved for contemporary persons Israel's concern for a holy community. Those who have studied that book will recall that it is in large measure concerned with how Israel can relate to God, who is holy. Many of the same concerns reappear in chapters 5 and 6 of Numbers. *First,* Levitical leadership sought to maintain the holiness of the community by putting every "unclean" person outside the camp (5:1-4). Ritual uncleanness precluded accessibility to God, while simultaneously alienating other persons because of its contagious power. Whatever the source—whether leprosy or persons with a discharge or unclean from contact with the dead—both male and female were put outside the camp.

Second, the holy character of the community was maintained through the reconciliation of those who may have wronged another (vv. 5-11). Not only was confession required, but both restitution and indemnification were necessary. The specific nature of the offense is not stated, other than reference to "any of the sins that men commit by breaking faith with the LORD." Yet the demand for restitution suggests that in some way the offense was directed against other persons. Note, for example, "But if the man has no kinsman to whom restitution may be made . . ." (v. 8). This stipulation parallels Leviticus 6:1-7 and is especially significant because of the elements of restitution and indemnification which were required as accompaniments of confession.

Third, in ways consistent with their culture, ancient Israel sought to maintain the fidelity of marital bonds. This they did in the present instance (5:11-31) through the ordeal which could be prescribed for wives of suspicious husbands. From a modern perspective, the passage is male dominated and chauvinistic. Yet, like a treasure in an earthen vessel, the passage affirms the sanctity of marriage. The passage presupposes the reality of a "spirit" that may dominate an individual, in this instance a "spirit of jealousy" that might come upon the husband (v. 14). In such cases the wife was brought to the priest, who administered a drink; and if the woman became ill, she was guilty. If she was unaffected, she was declared innocent (vv. 19-31). The objective nature of curses is graphically underscored in the practice of writing the curse, which had a unique way of objectifying the curse. But more than this, the drink prepared by the priest was poured over the curses so that he might wash the curses "off into the water of bitterness" (v. 23).

Fourth, the presence of persons uniquely related to the Lord such as the Nazirites (6:1-21) was yet another way by which Israel demonstrated the holiness of the community. The Nazirite might be "either a man or a woman" who made a special vow to separate himself/ herself to the Lord for a specified period of time. Such periods of dedication might be for a lifetime or for limited periods (v. 13). The word Nazirite is from a Hebrew verb which means to dedicate, consecrate, or separate. When one recalls that holy/holiness in Hebrew also meant to be separate, one may immediately see the relationship between the Nazirite and the holy life—that is, a life separated to God. Three acts of abstention uniquely marked the life of the Nazirite. He/she rejected all wine and strong drink, and even refused to eat anything "produced by the grapevine, not even the seeds or the skins." Prohibition of wine and strong drink was related to the process of fermentation; and, in turn, Israel's attitude toward leaven or anything fermented, even fruit-honey (cf. Lev. 2:11). The association of leaven with evil became traditional in biblical religion.

Also, as a part of the vow of separation, the Nazirite refused to use a razor on his head. At the conclusion of the vow the Nazirite shaved his head and put the hair on the fire of the peace offering (v. 18). The hair, like the blood, may have symbolized the life of a person.

The third stipulation for the Nazirite was separation from a dead body (vv. 6-12). The uncleanness of death is well established in the Old Testament, especially in the regulations of Leviticus and Numbers. While death may later have been reinterpreted with positive connotations, early Israel experienced no such affirmation of death. Life, not death, was affirmed in the Old Testament; and Israel never celebrated as did Egypt the anticipation of death. The New Testament also affirms life, and does so ultimately in the triumphant note of resurrection. For Christian believers, "The last enemy to be destroyed is death" (1 Cor. 15:26). With the resurrection of the body, "then shall come to pass the saying that is written: 'Death is swallowed up in victory' " (1 Cor. 15:54). The present-day candor and openness with which people both discuss and experience death is healthy. But for the Christian such openness to death is grounded in the affirmation of life, not in the affirmation of death. Death remains the last enemy to be destroyed, conquered by Christ who gives victory.

Through these stipulations persons in ancient Israel manifested their devotion, their separation from that which stood over against the Lord. Yet the focus was not so much on the separation from these three realities as it was on their dedication to the Lord. Their consecration was not an ascetic separation but rather an expression of loyalty to God in which such forms of abstinence were illustrative of a larger commitment of life to God.

Although contemporary believers manifest the holiness of their community through different forms than did Israel, the principle remains implicit for all. They maintained a holy community, dedicated to the Lord and to those ways of life which affirm one's relationship to him and to other believers. For Israel this claim on life manifested itself through common practices of their culture and time: attitudes toward unclean persons, the repayment of others for wrong, the discernment of marital infidelity, and symbolic dedication through the life-styles of persons such as the Nazirites. The challenge for present-day believers is to discover legitimate life-styles today which will testify to the nature of our relationship to God. They need to maintain the holiness of their relationship to God, not only as individuals but as communities.

Mediating the divine blessing (6:22-27).—It is significant that an extended statement on the holiness of the community should be followed directly by the priestly blessing. Religious leaders are mediators of divine blessing: "The LORD bless you and keep you:/The LORD make his face to shine upon you, and be gracious to you:/The LORD lift up his countenance upon you, and give you peace." Yet this is no blessing to be ritually shared irrespective of the worshiper who receives it. Who are those who discover in life this quality of benediction? Only those with the Lord's name on their lives, with all that phrase so richly implies, may experience life as benediction.

Responding to God's Presence (7:1 to 10:10)

Assuming the centrality of God's presence for the worshiping community, how shall persons respond to his presence (cf. Ex. 33:14)? In this passage are six responses which the community makes to the reality of divine presence.

Responding through dedicatory gifts (7:1-89).—Just as the concept of gift was an early reason for sacrifice, and as Israel continued to give herself symbolically through the burnt offering, so the gift remained a primary way of conveying oneself to God. As Paul later was to suggest in the context of the collection for the saints in Jerusalem: "I seek not what is yours but you" (2 Cor. 12:14). Gifts are the medium for transporting oneself to widely varying places and persons. Like money, they are a medium of exchange by which one communicates oneself. There were two facets of the offering made by the leaders of Israel. First, they brought oxen and carts to be used in transporting the tabernacle, a common but necessary gift. Second, each of the twelve tribes gave through its designated leader silver, gold, and appropriate elements for offering sacrifice. The offering was "for the dedication of the altar." The inventory of the gifts identified the magnitude of their giving, but even more the depth of their commitment.

On occasion in modern churches a note of apology emerges in urging others to give to some specific aspect of the church's ministry or to some other worthy cause. But historically, giving has always been an appropriate response to God. Through the gift a person is able to transmit himself or herself. Giving also leads to a growing maturity. Again, giving is a sure means of avoiding the introverted, selfish life. Giving probes as deeply as any other experience into the true nature of a person and what his or her ultimate loyalties are.

Responding through furnishing the sanctuary (8:1-4).—Throughout the instructions for creating the priest's garments there is the phrase "for glory and beauty" (Ex. 28:2,40). There is a place for glory and beauty in the sanctuary of God. Worship appeals to the full range of one's senses, including the aesthetic. The lamps of the sanctuary fulfilled at least three functions: *aesthetic,* for they were beautiful; and *practical,* lighting the otherwise dark holy place; and *symbolic,* for the light was related to the light/darkness theme of Old Testament religion. So Israel responded to the Lord's presence by appropriately furnishing the sanctuary.

Responding through dedicating the Lord's servants (8:5-26).— Responding to the centrality of the Lord's presence leads to the dedication of those who serve through the sanctuary, the Levites. The ceremony of dedication involved ritual cleansing, shaving the entire body, and offering the appropriate sacrifice. Cleansed, symbolically giving their lives to God, forgiven, and renewed in relationship with God through sacrifice, they were set apart for the Lord's service. For twenty-five years, from age twenty-five to fifty, they were to share a ministry with the priests as servants of the sanctuary.

Responding through worship: the second Passover (9:1-14).— People also respond to the centrality of God's presence by remembering his mighty acts of deliverance as Israel did at the time of Passover. While at Sinai, Israel celebrated the Passover for the second time. But this passage not only records this historical bit of information; it became the context for establishing an alternative date for Passover. Those contaminated by death could not celebrate Passover with the community, and in response to this problem there emerged the provision that in such cases one might observe the Passover one month later. Through the change of the date there is the implied suggestion that it is the act of worship and not the mechanics of date which is of fundamental importance. Such an emphasis is consistent with Jesus' later affirmation that man was not made for the sabbath but that the sabbath was made for man (cf. Mark 2:27). So today worship remains an appropriate way of responding to the presence of God. For worship is both proclamation and response—proclaiming the reality of God and responding to that presence.

Responding through following the Lord's leadership: the fiery cloud (9:15-23).—During the wilderness period the Lord's presence was often symbolized through cloud and fire (cf. Ex. 13:21-22). When the tabernacle was erected, for example, "Then the cloud covered the tent of meeting, and the glory of the LORD filled the tabernacle" (Ex. 40:34). The same terminology is used to describe the Lord's presence in the Temple Solomon constructed (cf. 1 Kings 8:11). The emphasis on the fiery cloud here directly parallels Exodus 40:36-38 and has the same intention of symbolizing the Lord's presence while simultaneously affirming Israel's response in following the Lord's leadership.

Responding through remembering: the trumpet of God (10:1-10).—This stipulation focuses on the creation of the silver trumpets used for summoning the congregation and for breaking camp, as well as for sounding an alarm. But the trumpets were also used to assemble people for worship. Apart from those functional uses, the trumpets "shall serve you for remembrance before your God" (v. 10). The object of that remembrance is not specified, and one can only surmise that it related to the wilderness experience. So in later Israel when one heard the trumpet summoning people to worship, they were to remember the calls of the trumpet in the wilderness—indeed, all that the Lord had done during that traumatic period. The call to worship is a call to remember the Lord, to remember all that he has done for his people who worship him. But the trumpet may also have symbolized their calling on the Lord when a needy people were besieged by an enemy.

Of course, modern believers are not expected to imitate all the patterns of ancient worship, but they need to hear in this ancient word a contemporary challenge to respond to the Lord's presence in creative ways related to their own culture and time. There is still a response to be made in *giving, furnishing the sanctuary, dedicating oneself* to the service of God, *worshiping* the Lord through a spiritual commitment, *following* the Lord's leadership, and *remembering* what God has done for us.

In summary, the scene set at Sinai concludes with Numbers 10:10; and from that point the narratives which describe the wilderness migration emerge. But in describing those months at Sinai, the book of Numbers focuses on the centrality of God's presence. Like the tabernacle in the midst of the camp, there is a central place for God in the whole of life. Like an enlarging series of concentric circles, that theme moves outward to include all aspects of Israel's being.

Rebelling Against the Lord
10:11 to 20:13

Israel's migration from Sinai to Paran was an experience characterized by faith and unfaith, loyalty and disloyalty, fidelity and rebellion. As every person has his or her shadowed side, so there was a shadowed side to Israel's experience with the Lord in the wilderness. On occasion her faith was resplendent and dynamic. Again, it gave way to despair, futility, and overt rebellion. Within the biblical literature this double tradition prevailed. Prophets saw in the period of wandering an experience with God comparable to the honeymoon shared by a newly married couple: "I remember the devotion of your youth, your love as a bride, how you followed me in the wilderness, in a land not sown" wrote the prophet Jeremiah (2:1; cf. Hos. 9:10). When Israel's hope for the future became the thrust of prophetic contemplation, on occasion it too took the form of a new exodus and a new leading through the wilderness (cf. Hos. 2:16; Jer. 31:31 ff.; Ezek. 20:32-44). But especially did Isaiah's eschatology reflect the form of a new exodus and a new wilderness experience: "When you pass through the waters I will be with you; and through the rivers, they shall not overwhelm you; when you walk through fire you shall not be burned, and the flame shall not consume you" (Isa. 43:2). But intertwined with such positive attitudes toward the wilderness was the awareness of rebellion as a primary characteristic of Israel during the periods of both wilderness and settlement.

This second major division of the book describes the migration from Sinai to Paran. But it is more than merely a story of that migration; there are also fidelity and rebellion. We can see them as: Israel *responding* to the Lord's leadership (10:11 to 12:16), *forfeiting* the Lord's promise (13:1 to 14:25), *rebelling* against the Lord's ministers (15:1 to 19:22), and *preempting* the Lord's power (20:1-13).

Responding to the Lord's Leadership (10:11 to 12:16)

How did Israel respond during the migration from Sinai to the wilderness of Paran? At first the people followed the Lord's guidance, but this commitment in faith soon dissipated and they began complaining against life's circumstances. Yet the narrative closes with a gracious portrait of Moses as the man for others, sharing the gift of leadership as well as God's Spirit and physical provision. But those qualities stood in marked contrast to Miriam and Aaron coveting Moses' role as the Lord's unique leader. So two sets of polarities form the structure for this part of the book: collectively, there are the contrasts between following and complaining; individually, one sees the marked contrast between sharing and coveting.

Following the Lord's Guidance (10:11-36)

Pioneers were persons who both willed to let go and willed to go on. Neither pleasant memories from the past nor fears of the future could keep them from going forward. Israel willed both to let go of what lay behind her in Egypt and Sinai and to go on under God's leadership mediated through Moses.

Willing to let go (10:11-32).—For eleven months Israel had remained at Sinai, engaged in covenant making and preparation for the journey beyond (cf. Ex. 19:1; Num. 10:11). It had been fourteen months and twenty days since the Exodus out of Egypt (v. 11) and nineteen days following the census (Num. 1:1), but the day of departure had arrived. As the book of Deuteronomy records the memory of Moses' challenge, "The LORD our God said to us in Horeb, 'You have stayed long enough at this mountain' " (Deut. 1:6). The future belongs only to those who will to let go of the past.

Two significant elements marked Israel's departure from Sinai. First,

God gave the sign which previously had been promised. The cloud above the tabernacle "was taken up" (cf. Ex. 40:34-38; Num. 9:15-23). Second, the line of march previously described (Num. 2:1-34) was implemented, with the tabernacle appropriately fixed in the midst of the people. Note, however, that the ark went before the people during their journey of three days (v. 33). By this means the writer emphasized the Lord's leadership, since he was symbolically envisioned as enthroned above the ark between the cherubim. In this way the holiness of God was emphasized as the Tabernacle was carried in the midst of the people, protecting the holiness associated with the tent of meeting. In the blending of these two interpretations of the line of march, both God's holiness and his leadership were stressed.

How difficult it must have been for the people to leave the holy mountain where the Lord had appeared and the requirements of covenant life had been assumed. For persons who thought of God as identified with a high place such as Sinai or another fixed sanctuary, the concept of a movable place of worship and the portable ark symbolizing the presence of a God who could go with the people was something new. It was an exciting venture to respond to the possibility that God was not limited to one place but could be with persons wherever they went. From Sinai and afterward the Lord was the God who was uniquely with his people (cf. Ex. 3:14).

Willing to go on (10:33-36).—More is required of believers than that they let go of their past. As with Israel, letting go presupposes going on to that which claims one's life out of the future. Believing that God has gone before us into the future and that it is from there that he calls us, our pilgrimage in faith becomes future oriented. Before leaving Sinai, Moses spoke to his father-in-law, Hodab, known also as Jethro in other communities in Israel (cf. Ex. 4:18). Hodab (Jethro) declined the invitation to accompany Moses (v. 30), but in so inviting him Moses clarified Israel's commitment to God's future. First, "we are setting out for the place of which the LORD said, 'I will give it to you' " (v. 29a). Second, to accompany those bound up with God's purposes "will do you good; for the LORD has promised good to Israel" (v. 29b).

Complaining Against Life's Circumstances (11:1-9)

For those who assume that the wilderness experience was one of bliss, there is the quick reminder that murmuring against Moses as against the Lord was a primary characteristic of that experience. No sooner had Israel set out from Sinai than the people began to complain about the adversities experienced during the pilgrimage.

Complaining about life's troubles (11:1-3).—What Israel's "misfortunes" were, one can only speculate. Food was a primary concern, and perhaps those early pilgrims were less enthusiastic about a lengthy journey beyond Sinai than in the promised "three days journey" referred to so often in the Exodus narrative. Conflict with local or regional tribes also plagued the pilgrims (cf. Ex. 17:8-13), and even Miriam and Aaron chafed under Moses' leadership (Num. 12:1-8). The Hebrew word translated "misfortunes" has the basic connotations of calamity, distress, misery, or injury. Whatever the specific nature of the misfortunes, Israel discovered early in her pilgrimage what some never accept: that commitment in faith to the Lord brings no immunity from hardship, trial, and difficulty. Later the apostle Paul learned through experience that "[God's] grace is sufficient for you, for my power is made perfect in weakness . . . I am content with weaknesses, insults, hardships, persecutions, and calamities; for when I am weak, then I am strong" (2 Cor. 12:9-10). But scarcely does a person begin the pilgrimage in faith before complaint about adversity arises.

Complaining about life's needs (11:4-9).—Facing the ultimate threat of starvation, Israel welcomed the manna with gratitude (cf. Ex. 16:13-21). As God's gift it came as a miracle in the midst of great need. But over a year had passed and the manna had become monotonous and wearisome. Now the people complained. Taking the gift of God for granted, Israel forgot that such elemental food had delivered them in their desperate need. Now they wanted more than the necessities: "the cucumbers, the melons, the leeks, the onions, and the garlic" (v. 5). But lest we criticize those pilgrims unduly, we might remember that such ingratitude is universal. Much later Jesus warned disciples about their inability to trust God for elemental needs of life (cf. Matt. 6:31-33).

Sharing the Lord's Gifts (11:10-35)

How does one deal with conflict and the complaints of committed persons like those early pilgrims in the wilderness? One might respond authoritatively, crushing the complaint, or at least driving it into internal submission. One might join the complainers, forfeiting one's leadership. Significantly, Moses did neither of these. Rather, he met conflict through the principle of shared or participatory leadership. Such leadership manifested itself in three ways: sharing leadership, God's Spirit, and provisions to meet human need.

Sharing the gift of leadership (11:10-25).—To what extent is leadership a gift? Within the community of faith is it not a gift in the sense of an entrusted responsibility? God had given to Moses the role of leader in Israel. It was the call of God (Ex. 3:1-6) which activated Moses' response to God, motivated him to return to Egypt, and validated his ministry to the Hebrews (Ex. 3:13). But leadership which is effective cannot remain singular, restricted, and limited in scope. Moses' frustration echoes the desperation of many leaders in every generation who unwisely adopt a singular view of leadership; he complained: "I am not able to carry all this people alone; the burden is too heavy for me."

Out of this context there emerged the concept of the seventy elders of Israel who fulfilled a shared ministry with Moses. Another version of this development circulated in Northern Israel and appears in Exodus 18:13-27, which ascribed the creation of the seventy to the counsel of Jethro. But the result is the same in both narratives: Shared ministry is a responsible way to meet the multiplicity of needs confronted by the people of God. No one person, not even a Moses, can perform all the ministry or meet all the needs. Yet not every person has the grace and the strength of character necessary to begin sharing leadership.

Sharing the gift of God's Spirit (11:26-30).—The fundamental meaning of Spirit in the Old Testament might well be described as God's energizing power. The Spirit was at work in creation and afterward in both nonhuman and human dimensions of the world. Here, for example, the seventy persons selected to share Moses' ministry were empowered by the Spirit.

Among the elders of Israel, however, there were two, Eldad and Medad, who had remained in the camp. When God's Spirit came on them, they also prophesied as did the other elders. When a young man reported this, Joshua counseled Moses to forbid them. "But Moses said to him, 'Are you jealous for my sake? Would that all the LORD'S people were prophets, that the LORD would put his spirit upon them!'" (v. 29). It ill behooves any servant of God to be jealous of others who may also know the energizing power of God. The magnitude of Moses' stature both as a leader and as a person was reflected in his ability to share with grace the gift of God's Spirit. Such conduct stands in marked contrast with a leader who is jealous of his leadership, its origins, and its prerogatives.

Sharing the gift of God's provisions (11:31-35).—In contrast to the Exodus account of the quail, which assumes that the provision of flesh and the bread testify to the uniqueness of God (Ex. 16:12), the account in Numbers is characterized by judgment on the people. No sooner had they eaten the quail than a plague smote the people. In its unique way Numbers stresses that the original gift of manna was adequate and that the plague which followed eating the quail was in some manner related to the grumbling of the people (11:1-9). The point seems clear: In however elemental a form, God provides for human need. Sharing God's elemental gift enables one to meet such need adequately. This passage is not a polemic against those who seek more than the bare necessities of life. But it does affirm that when the elemental needs of life have been met, no one is justified in complaining about the nature of God's gifts.

Coveting the Lord's Representative (12:1-16)

That coveting the leadership role of another is a common failure is reflected in the attitude of Miriam and Aaron toward Moses. Another illustration of such covetousness is the attempt by Absalom to undermine David's leadership (cf. 2 Sam. 15:1-12).

Criticism and covetousness (12:1-3).—Critical of Moses' marriage to a Cushite woman, Miriam and Aaron not only spoke against that action but also coveted Moses' leadership role: "Has the LORD indeed spoken only through Moses? Has he not spoken through us also?" One might interpret this as a statement on the breadth of God's revelation through a variety of persons. But this does not seem to be the intent of the passage. Rather, criticism and jealousy permeate the narrative.

Although Cush was the ancient name of a territory south of Egypt, Cushan is used of Midianites (cf. Hab. 3:7). Here the reference is not to an Ethiopian but to the Midianitess, Zipporah, whom Moses married while in exile (cf. Ex. 2:21). The narrative may reflect a later and priestly antipathy toward the non-Israelite wife of Moses. But the twin threats of criticism and covetousness still rage, whatever the era.

The uniqueness of personal relationship (12:4-8).—Through an appearance of the Lord, the uniqueness of Moses' relationship to him was reaffirmed. Although the Lord might speak to prophets through vision and dream, not so with Moses. With him the Lord spoke directly (v. 8). Through such symbolic yet authentic language the writer made clear the uniqueness of God's revelation mediated through Moses. The question set before Miriam and Aaron is appropriate for each believer. If the Lord's revelation is unique, why were they "not afraid to speak against my servant Moses?" If one believes in the uniqueness of God's revelation, why does one fail to take it seriously and to make decisions which reflect one's understanding of God? The question remains rhetorical, calling each person to accountability.

The grace of unthreatened leadership (12:9-16).—Leadership which is secure and unthreatened confronts criticism with grace and dignity. In the face of God's judgment of Miriam for her presumptuous action, Moses interceded for her: "Heal her, O God, I beseech thee" (v. 13). A less secure and threatened person might well have supported the judgment of a critic. But not Moses. Even for those who criticized him he sought God's benediction. There is a mark of grace and serenity in Moses' action not unlike that of Jesus on the cross (Luke 23:34). Strength and character of leadership are revealed in one's ability to respond to criticism with grace as opposed to condescension, and especially in the ability to seek the welfare of those who criticize and covet.

Forfeiting the Lord's Promise (13:1 to 14:45)

The familiar narrative of the spies sent to Canaan forms another facet of the larger rebellion motif in the wilderness experience. While admitting the goodness of God's gift, which would have fulfilled the promise made so long ago to the patriarchs, the majority of the spies still concluded that the land could not be taken. Through their negative response to this opportunity, they forfeited the Lord's promise. Their modern descendants continue to waver in the context of challenging opportunities which beckon them toward God's future. Failing to take the risks inevitably attached to opportunity reminds us of the homely but suggestive observation of Logan Pearsall Smith: "What is more mortifying than to feel that you've missed the plum for want of courage to shake the tree?"

Exploring the Promise of God (13:1-24)

Twelve persons, one from each of the tribes of Israel, were selected to spy out the land of Canaan. They were charged to go throughout the land, from the Negeb to the hill country, and to report on the people, the goodness of the land, and the cities. They moved throughout the land, from south to north, and brought back from the Valley of Eshcol (i.e., "cluster") pomegranates and a giant cluster of grapes which two spies carried on a pole. It was obvious that it was a good land, fulfilling God's promises both to the patriarchs and to the immediate generation.

Responding to the Lord's Promise (13:25-33)

The character of the land made it obviously desirable. Figuratively, its richness was described as flowing with milk and honey. But the people who lived there constituted a liability. Despite the report of the people who occupied the land, the counsel of Caleb from the tribe of Judah was clear: "Let us go up at once, and occupy it; for we are well able." The opposition of the majority was equally clear: "They brought to the people of Israel an evil report of the land." So a faithless majority ruled without being right. Their lack of faith committed Israel to another generation of useless wandering.

Complaining Against the Lord's Promise (14:1-10)

Facing the reportedly impregnable land of Canaan, the people succumbed to despair, crying and weeping. Their frustration was soon vented on Moses and Aaron. But their anger reached beyond them to the purposes of God. Facing such circumstances, they would have preferred death in Egypt or in the wilderness to reaching the border of a Promised Land but finding it impossible to conquer. Complaining soon led to a more direct proposal: "Let us choose a captain, and go back to Egypt" (v. 4). Joshua of the tribe of Ephraim (cf. also "Hoshea," 13:8) and Caleb from Judah argued that the land was exceedingly good, and that if the Lord delighted in them he would bring them into the land. This report was met with open hostility, and "all the congregation said to stone them with stones" (v. 10). So it was that the grandeur of God's promise and the splendor of a new opportunity foundered through lack of faith. It was true that Canaanites were entrenched in the land and that they were able to defend that land fiercely. But the untried ingredient was never injected into Israel's response: the reality of God's providence undergirded by his power in history to achieve his purposes. Lacking faith to act on that reality, the people were too weak to expect anything but failure.

Interceding for Faithless Persons (14:11-25)

When the Lord proposed that he disinherit Israel and make of Moses "a nation greater and mightier than they" (v. 12), a lesser person might have succumbed to the temptation of advancing his interest at the expense of another's misfortune. But not Moses. Again, he manifested the charitable spirit and the supportive mood. For Moses interceded with the Lord, saying that the Egyptians would hear that the Lord had failed his people in their need, implying that the God of Israel was powerless to fulfill his promises (vv. 13-15). Responding to Moses' intercession, the Lord agreed that he would not destroy the people. But simultaneously he affirmed that none of those who had continually refused his leadership would ever see the Promised Land. Only Caleb and Joshua would be exempt.

Reaping the Results of Faithlessness (14:26-45)

One year for each day it took to spy out the land, forty years, the people would wander as nomads through the wilderness (vv. 26-35). Of those twenty years of age upward who had murmured against the Lord, not one would enter the land except Caleb and Joshua. But prior to the effect of that judgment, those who brought back the evil report were killed through a plague (v. 37). Too late, the people then sought to take the land; and in an abortive effort to attack the Canaanites, they were defeated and pursued into the wilderness. Israel failed to live up to their opportunities and resources. But without faith commitment grounded in one's relationship to God, no one is able to live up to life's opportunities. But with him—that's the secret—with him, from plains to hill country, the land and all that is symbolically conveyed thereby can belong to faithful pilgrims in any age.

Rebelling Against the Lord's Ministers (15:1 to 19:22)

Throughout this section the rebellion motif continues, along with some intertwined collections of stipulations governing worship and the sanctuary. Although these disparate elements came from different periods of time in Israel's pilgrimage, they are bound together by a common focus on rebellion. At times such rebellion manifested itself openly toward leadership. On other occasions there are narratives which recount the violation of stipulations but apart from specific reference to religious leaders. Within the larger section there are emphases on *regulating* the Lord's worship (15:1-32), *violating* the Lord's Day (15:32-36), *remembering* the Lord's command (15:37-41), *rebelling* against the Lord's leader (16:1-50), and *validating* the Lord's ministers (17:1 to 19:22).

Regulating the Worship of the Lord (15:1-31)

Miscellaneous laws related to sacrifice and offerings comprise the primary content of this passage. Attention is given to guidelines for such acts of worship and to persons who sin, whether unintentionally or deliberately.

Guidelines for worship (15:1-21).—Although differing in detail from stipulations in the book of Leviticus, the guidelines have the character of Levitical regulations. Their intention was to specify the attendant offerings that were required with a sacrifice. Such offerings had three ingredients: fine flour, oil, and wine. Given the earlier prohibition of fermented substances, the introduction of wine is unusual and may suggest a much later period of time than the wilderness and early Israel for the introduction of the practice. The quantity of the offering varied with the type of sacrifice (cf. vv. 4,6,9). A "stranger" (probably an alien living in Israel rather than one merely passing through the land) could sacrifice (v. 14), but should he do so the stipulations were the same as for an Israelite. Also, when persons ate the food of the land, it was required that they "present an offering to the LORD."

Unintentional and deliberate sin (15:22-31).—In the case of "un-

witting" (v. 24) sins or unintentional sins, appropriate means were
specified for the forgiveness of the entire congregation. Sin was contagious, as was holiness, and the sin of one person improperly offering
a sacrifice affected the larger community. The specifications for such
a sacrifice were given (vv. 27-29) and the assurance of forgiveness
pledged both to native Israelite and to stranger (v. 26). But in the
case of deliberate sin, sin with a "high hand," there was no sacrifice.
Rather, one was cut off from the people, a phrase which probably
implied death. Those who despised the word of the Lord and broke
his commandment bore their own iniquity (v. 31), for there no longer
remained a sacrifice for those who sinned with a high hand. Such
an emphasis was a forerunner of the insight in the book of Hebrews,
"For if we sin deliberately after receiving the knowledge of the truth,
there no longer remains a sacrifice for sins, but a fearful prospect of
judgment" (Heb. 10:26-27; cf. 6:1-8).

Violating the Lord's Day (15:32-36)

The seriousness with which Israel accepted covenant requirements
is shown clearly in the stoning of the man found picking up sticks
on the sabbath. The action in itself was trivial and perhaps necessary,
whatever use he may have made of the sticks. It was the fact that
the Lord's Day had been usurped, not the nature of the action, that
made the action so serious. While no one would support death for
sabbath violation today, the seriousness with which Israel honored
God through the dedication of time and life is noteworthy.

Remembering the Lord's Command (15:37-41)

Memory plays its tricks on everyone. Those things we think we
will never forget are forgotten; even those things we want to forget
and should forget, too often we remember. Perhaps one of the most
serious threats believers face in their commitment to God is not that
of deliberate sin but the gnawing temptation to relegate the acts
and laws of God to the realm of the forgotten, even to forget what
the Lord has done in one's own life. As a deterrent to that threat,
the people of Israel were commanded to wear tassels with a cord of
blue on the corners of their garments (v. 40). Yet "remember" is a
far more dynamic concept in biblical Hebrew than in contemporary
English language. "Remember" did not mean merely to call to mind;
it also meant to act in light of a past commitment or experience.

For example, God "remembered" his covenant and came down to deliver Israel in Egypt (Ex. 2:24). So those who take the biblical revelation seriously are not only called to remember what God has done; they are called on to live out the commandments, to implement them in daily life.

Rebelling Against the Lord's Leader (16:1-50)

The narrative which describes the rebellion of Korah, Dathan, and Abiram sets the rebellion motif within the context of personal, willful rejection of leadership. The seriousness of this rebellion is clearly reflected in that 250 leaders and well-known men rose up against Aaron and Moses to insist: "You have gone too far" (v. 3).

The seriousness of the rebellion was reflected further in the truth inherent in the charge, "For all the congregation are holy . . . and the LORD is among them; why then do you exalt yourselves above the assembly of the LORD?" (v. 3). This issue continues as one of crucial import for the contemporary church: What is the relationship between traditional ministerial leadership and the concept of all persons as ministers? Is there legitimacy in the charge of the rebels? Many today would agree that all the congregation is holy; why should any one person or persons be singled out in a unique way as minister? Congregations need to resolve this issue lest extremists from both directions pull the congregation into the abyss of chaotic ineffectiveness.

The fundamental issue rested in the tension between the priests and the Levites. The Levites fomented the rebellion, aspiring to a priestly function. So the issue was further intensified. Not merely the congregation was holy, but the Levites as holy persons became the issue. By what right were the descendants of Aaron inheritors of a more superior role in ministry than the Levites? Stated in contemporary terms, the issue was one of "staff relationships." Inherent to the narrative was a time of conflict between the two groups; perhaps such conflict related to the centralization of worship or to developments during the exile. Whatever the focus, the issue was clear: "Would you seek the priesthood also?" (v. 10).

How was the issue resolved? Although, as a leader, Moses responded with grace and compassion in interceding for Miriam and Aaron (cf. 12:13) and later for the entire congregation (cf. 14:13-25), his response to rebellion was one of anger (v. 15). The rebellion was directed against

Moses as a "prince," but more than Moses was involved. The purpose of God was also involved, for it was his purpose to lead the congregation of Israel into Canaan: "Hereby you shall know that the LORD has sent me to do all these works, and that it has not been of my own accord" (v. 28).

Trial by ordeal determined that the Lord gave no support to the rebels. Moses challenged them to take censers and offer incense to the Lord (vv. 6-7). In this way all would determine readily and observably whether or not their usurpation of the priestly office had divine support. If the men died a common death, then Moses acknowledged that the Lord had not sent him and that his work had been at his own initiative. But they did not die a common death, for "the ground under them split asunder; and the earth opened its mouth and swallowed them up" (vv. 31-32). Consequently all Israel learned and remembered that "no one who is not a priest who is not of the descendants of Aaron, should draw near to burn incense before the Lord." Although it reflects a different theme, this narrative is akin to that of Nadab and Abihu, the sons of Aaron who violated the holiness of the sanctuary (Lev. 10:1-11).

But the last word in the narrative is one of grace, not of judgment. For when the people murmured against Moses and accused him of having killed the people of the Lord, the Lord threatened their destruction (vv. 41-45). But in this context the intercessory role of Moses reappeared. Although the plague killed many, the congregation was delivered through the intercession of a leader who could minister to others despite all criticism, hostility, and rebellion.

Validating the Lord's Ministers (17:1 to 19:22)

The narrative on Aaron's rod that budded (17:1-12) and the succeeding material on ministering for God's people (18:1 to 19:22) appear to have been placed at this juncture in the book as a means of validating the ministry of Aaron and Moses, indeed of all God's ministers. When the authenticity of ministry is questioned, its most significant validation rests with God as it reveals the fulfilling qualities of God's call and providence.

Refuting complainers: authenticating Aaron's ministry (17:1-12).—However one may understand the phenomenon itself, the budding of Aaron's rod had the effect of validating Aaron's ministry. More so, it spoke of the way in which ministerial validation inevitably rises from God's confirming acts. The test was of the same type as others in the Old Testament in which persons sought some physical sign of God's approval. Since nearly fifteen thousand persons had died from the plague (16:49) and two tribes had been involved (Levi and Reuben), the validation was needed. The rods were marked, one for each of the twelve tribes; and the rod of Levi was the one that sprouted, produced blossoms, and bore almonds (v. 8).

And what shall one say of a contemporary minister? Certainly, no one anticipates that his or her ministry should be validated in a like manner as in ancient Israel. But this is not to say that it should not be validated. Each person who claims to minister for God is called upon to give evidences of legitimate ministry. Although modern persons have no rod that blossoms and bears fruit, what are the authenticating marks of contemporary ministry?

Ministering for God's people (18:1 to 19:22).—Aware of their alienation from God, Israel lamented that they would surely perish (17:12-13). But to provide mediation between God and persons, the priests and Levites shared a ministry of reconciliation (18:1 ff.). Four aspects of that ministry emerge within the narrative.

First, the priests and Levites were called to a shared ministry, with each accountable to God for responsibilities at the worship center (vv. 1-7).

Second, supporting the ministry was the responsibility of the congregation through sacrifices and tithes offered at the worship center (vv. 8-24). For the priests, support came through the portion of the sacrifices and offerings designated for their use. For example, they received the offerings made to the Lord, together with other consecrated things. Those portions of sacrifices specified for the priests, together with the first fruit and firstborn; those also belonged to the priests. Consequently, the priests were to have no share in the land (v. 20). For the Levites, the tithe was given in return for their service at the tent of meeting (v. 21). Hence, neither were they to have an inheritance (v. 24).

Third, tithing by the Lord's ministers was presupposed (vv. 25-32). When the Levites received the tithe of the people, they were then to present an offering, "a tithe of the tithe" (v. 26), and it was to be of the "best" (v. 30). In such faithfulness the Levites would "bear no sin by reason of it" (v. 32). Religious leaders who fail to give as they encourage others to give are guilty. Although the practice was ancient, the principle is ever contemporary.

Fourth, delivering the Lord's people from uncleanness was a priestly role made possible through the ritual prescribed for removing uncleanness (19:1-22). Although the laws of clean and unclean relationships were a part of the further biblical revelation, they contained the positive concern that one should approach the Lord with a life cleansed of that which would separate one from God.

Preempting the Lord's Power (20:1-13)

Not even Moses was exempt from the erosive effects of rebellion. His action in striking the rock rather than addressing it as the Lord instructed ultimately precluded both his and Aaron's entrance into Canaan (v. 12). The locale of this event came to be known as Meribah (meaning "contention"), referring to the way in which the people contended with the Lord during the period of wandering between Sinai and Moab. The incident of the rock and the contention associated with it constitute an appropriate summation of Israel's attitude in the wilderness.

The narrative is like others in the Old Testament which describe the hunger and thirst that threatened Israel. Specifically, it is a parallel account of the event described in Exodus 17:2-7, where the name Meribah is explained in relation to the murmuring of the people before they reached Sinai.

The action of Moses shows the achievement of a worthy goal through questionable means. The point which the writer makes is not that the water was provided but that Moses usurped to himself the power of God. Priestly theology consistently emphasized that action must follow the proper ritual prescription; the Lord determines the pattern of action that the community of faith is to follow. A person might ask today what difference it made whether one struck the rock or addressed it on behalf of God. Water came forth anyway. But for ancient persons it mattered greatly that the action did not follow a prescribed, divine pattern. At another level, also, Moses' action reflected that of a person entrusted with greater and greater responsibility until finally he forgot that the power to act is delegated. As many of his successors, Moses forgot that he was the mediator of God's power; the power was not his apart from God. Further, the narrative explains how the place name, "Meribah," originated and also why neither Moses nor Aaron entered the land of Canaan, the Promised Land.

Achieving the Lord's Purposes
20:14 to 36:13

It is one thing to dream a dream but quite another to will its fulfillment and to overcome obstacles to its realization. But Israel did both. Inspired by God, she dreamed a dream larger than one could have imagined apart from the promises of God. Sustained by God, Israel both willed its realization and triumphed over obstacles set in the pathway of that dream. The three stages of Israel's pilgrimage through the wilderness were climaxed by achievement of the promise made so long before to Abraham. There would be both a land and a people, as promised to the patriarchs. Preparatory to leaving Sinai, the centrality of the Lord for the pilgrimage was affirmed (1:1 to 10:10), yet Israel consistently rebelled against the Lord (10:11 to 20:13). But those purposes were not to be denied, and this section of the pilgrimage narrative records the final drama in the realization of God's purposes. Such an achievement as Israel realized involved triumphing over life's obstacles, listening to a new voice, preparing for a new life, and living in the land.

Triumphing over Life's Obstacles (20:14 to 21:35)

In the wilderness experience Israel soon learned what many never learn: that faith brings no immunity from hardships, trials, and difficulties. Triumph, not escape, is the more appropriate response to obstacles—whether at the sea or in the wilderness, yesterday or today. So in the final stage of the pilgrimage to the Promised Land, Israel confronted one difficulty after another. Little wonder that the people complained and became impatient (21:4). While the form and structure of crises may change, and do change from one era to another, the reality of life's obstacles remains constant. Persons may not experience today the same kind of trouble that plagued Israel, but the obstacles that plagued Israel are universal maladies: the loss of brotherly consideration, the loss of primary leadership, the hostility of warring tribes, the pain of natural disaster, and the conflict of regional enemies.

The Loss of Brotherly Consideration (20:14-21)

It may appear strange to identify Israel and Edom as brothers, but they were (v. 14). Their heritage encompassed the conflict between Jacob and Esau, just as their lineage flowed from Abraham, their common father. Such a conflict motif continued throughout history and manifests itself again in the twentieth century in Arab-Israeli tensions. To march from Kadesh to the area west of Canaan, Israel needed to cross Edomite territory. Although full assurances were given that no damage to the countryside would occur (v. 17), Edom refused to permit the Israelites to travel the international highway that served as an avenue to Egypt for centuries. No appeal by Israel on any basis was acceptable (vv. 14-17). From the beginning there was little brotherly consideration between those two brothers. Israel's first obstacle was the alienation of persons. Between Israel and the Promised Land lay not only the barren wastes of the semiarid desert land, but the ruptured personal relationships of two people. A primary obstacle to overcome in achieving the purposes of God remains the loss of brotherly consideration flowing from personal alienation and the disintegration of relationships.

The Death of Primary Leadership (20:22-29)

Just at the time when leadership was most needed, the Lord revealed that Aaron would not enter the land promised to the people of Israel. Although one might assume that the judgment for presuming on the power of God in striking the rock at Meribah involved only Moses (20:12), the personal pronoun "you" in that text is plural; "you [plural] did not believe in me, to sanctify me in the eyes of the people." So the death of Aaron was related to an earlier refusal to follow the Lord's revelation, and he died at Mount Hor (v. 28). That Aaron filled a role of primary leadership is reflected in the statement that "all the house of Israel wept for Aaron thirty days" (v. 29). Coupled with the trauma of death was the awareness of divine judgment, to say nothing of the loss of a significant leader. At the precise time when

Israel entered the final phase of the pilgrimage, Moses' faithful associate died. This too was an obstacle to be overcome in achieving the
purpose of God.

The Hostility of Warring Tribes (21:1-3)

Although it is impossible to locate "Atharim" precisely, it probably
was close to the Negeb or slightly southeast of the lower reaches of
the Dead Sea. The Negeb itself is a nebulous term, however, and
we can be sure only that a Canaanite king, anticipating a foray by
Israel into Canaan, took the offensive and attacked the Israelites. Some
of the Israelites were taken captive; but when Moses led Israel to
take a vow to the Lord, they defeated the Canaanites. The vow may
have had other components, but minimally it embodied a commitment to destroy utterly the cities of the Canaanites. The vow was
fulfilled and the site of the destruction was named "Hormah," meaning
"destruction." The place itself may have been as far into Canaan as
the cities of Beersheba, Gerar, and Debir.

The phrase "utterly destroy" translates a Hebrew verb that means
to put to the ban in the religious sense of dedicating something to
God by obliterating the person or object. Thus, far more was involved
than the mere extermination of the Canaanites. The phrase suggests
the reality of holy war, especially the prescription that all persons,
animals, and property be destroyed. So another obstacle to Israel was
confronted and overcome.

The Pain of Natural Disaster (21:4-9)

Reference to "Red Sea" in verse 4 focuses on the Gulf of Akaba,
which is often so described in the Old Testament, but one should
not confuse this with the sea the Israelites crossed when coming out
of Egypt. The Hebrew term can be translated "sea of reeds" and
apparently referred to different geographical areas. In an effort to
circumvent the Edomites, the people became impatient and complained against Moses' leadership. As a judgment fiery serpents bit
the people, but Moses interceded with the Lord on behalf of the
people.

It was in this context that the Lord commanded Moses to make
the bronze serpent, placing it on a pole with the exhortation that
all who looked on it would live (v. 9). This experience may well have

been related to the bronze serpent that was associated with worship in Jerusalem until the time of Hezekiah. During his reform he "broke in pieces the bronze serpent that Moses had made" (2 Kings 18:4). The passage found its ultimate fulfillment, however, in the New Testament: "And as Moses lifted up the serpent in the wilderness, so must the Son of man be lifted up, that whoever believes in him may have eternal life" (John 3:14-15). For those beset by rebellion and sin, disconsolate and disenchanted because of the obstacles, the message remains: Look up, and in faith find life rising out of travail.

The Ambiguity of an Unknown Future (21:10-20)

The people of God are a pilgrim people, destined always to be on the way. They never reach the point of thinking that God has no more tomorrows to challenge them onward. So, with Israel in the wilderness, the future was always open; and that openness was uncertain and ambiguous. Note the words of movement: "set out"; "from there they set out"; "and from there they continued"; "and from the wilderness they went on." Can you imagine the frustration and the discouragement of constantly pitching tents, only to break camp and begin again?

Yet in the sameness of their repetitious living, there was the pull of God's tomorrow. The call to follow him into the future prevailed, and Israel finally stood on the land promised so long before. But the pilgrimage was not without its ambiguity, for uncertainty is the inevitable accompaniment of a pilgrim set in history to achieve the purposes of God. Perhaps as threatening to Israel as the traditional enemies whom they encountered, the leadership they lost, and the fiery serpents that plagued them was the monotonous sameness of every tomorrow that seemed to get nowhere. Modern lives are challenged to triumph over the same kind of obstacle.

The Conflict with Regional Enemies (21:21-35)

In succession Israel defeated the king of Ammon, dispossessed the Amorites, and then conquered Bashan far to the north. Although the Moabites remained, all others were conquered and Israel "encamped in the plains of Moab beyond the Jordan at Jericho" (22:1). Obstacles had been overcome; it remained now only for Israel to cross the Jordan and dispossess those who held the land.

Listening to a New Voice (22:1 to 24:25)

These Balaam oracles have every evidence of being a separate literary collection designed to underscore the priority of the Lord over
those powers set against him. The oracles illustrate the way in which
persons may seek to manipulate religion for personal advantage. But
they emphasize no less strongly the fact that the Lord cannot be
manipulated, neither to curse one's enemies nor to bless oneself.
Throughout the oracles there is a consistent focus on listening to a
new voice, the voice of the Lord experienced through covenant relationships. Two primary themes constitute the fabric of the narrative:
manipulating the Lord's word as Balak sought to do and hearing the
Lord's word as Balaam did in four successive oracles. Those opposite
attitudes continue to challenge present-day believers.

Manipulating the Lord's Word (22:1-40)

Confronted by the encroaching hordes of Israelite settlers, Balak
the Moabite king sought recourse other than battle. Other kings had
sought to defeat the Israelites, but in turn each had been defeated.
Another strategy seemed wise. Why not enlist a prophetic-type person
to curse the Israelites?

Exploiting divine powers (22:1-6).—The acts of cursing and blessing were much more dynamic in early Old Testament times than
in contemporary religious experience. Both were more than mere
words; in releasing the curse or the blessing, a person released a unique
word with the power of its own fulfillment. For example, it was for
this reason that Isaac could not recall the blessing when he discovered
that he had mistakenly blessed his impostor son, Jacob. Both blessing
and curse had objective reality and could bring about their own fulfillment.

This attitude helps one to understand the dynamic conception of
the word: "So shall my word be that goes forth from my mouth;/it
shall not return to me empty,/but it shall accomplish that which I
purpose,/and prosper in the thing for which I sent it" (Isa. 55:11).
The same objective, inherent power also characterized the curse. One
needed, however, the right person to cast the blessing or the curse.
Balak found such an individual in the person of Balaam. He was not
identified as a worshiper of the Lord; nor was he related to Israelite
religion. But he did come from the regions of Israel's ancestors; and,

more importantly, the Lord revealed himself through Balaam. The effort to manipulate the divine word is clear: "Come now, curse this people for me . . . ; for I know that he whom you bless is blessed, and he whom you curse is cursed" (v. 6). When confronted by circumstances beyond their control, some people are tempted to manipulate divine relationships. To make religion serve one's own end, and to misuse sacred experiences is to misunderstand the character of the divine/human encounter.

Doing what God bids (22:7-20).—On two separate occasions the messengers of Balak approached Balaam. First, with "the fees for divination in their hand," they came asking that he return with them to Moab. Before responding Balaam sought divine instruction, and the Lord commanded Balaam neither to go with the men nor to curse Israel. A second time the representatives of Balak came, and again Balaam sought the divine will. No matter what Balak might offer, Balaam "could not go beyond the command of the LORD" (v. 18). Although not an Israelite prophet, Balaam obviously was portrayed according to prophetic-type persons of ancient Mesopotamia. Indeed, much of his conduct was described in patterns consistent with early Israelite prophets (cf. 1 Sam. 9:6-10). He remains even for contemporary readers an idealized figure whose action was controlled by the divine will.

Speaking what God says (22:21-40).—Not only are believers to do what God bids, but faithful disciples are also those who speak what God says. The story of Balaam and his ass not only entertained early Israelites but also embodied theological truth, as did other parabolic-type stories of the Old Testament which portrayed plants and animals speaking. When Balaam was apparently permitted by God, he went with the princes of Moab. But as he rode, "the angel of the Lord" stood in his way with a drawn sword. Because the ass could see the angel, she avoided him by turning aside, much to Balaam's discomfort and frustration. After striking the ass three times, Balaam was reprimanded by the ass (vv. 28-30), as the ass insisted that never had she previously turned aside as in these instances (vv. 23,25,27). In the larger context of the narrative the implication is obvious: There must have been some reason for that surprising action. Only then did Balaam recognize that the angel of the Lord was confronting him, suggesting a veiled appearance of the Lord to Balaam, who was insensitive to the divine presence.

When Balaam sensed the anger of the Lord, he acknowledged his sin (v. 34) and volunteered to return to his own land. But the Lord permitted him to continue his journey with a single stipulation: "Only the word which I bid you, that shall you speak" (v. 35). Balaam's response to Balak was controlled by the divine word. To that point Balaam's fault had been that of failing to recognize the Lord's presence; he would not compound that sin by failing to speak the Lord's word. This was later confirmed when Balaam refused to claim for himself the power that belonged only to God: "Have I now any power at all to speak anything? The word that God puts in my mouth, that must I speak" (v. 38).

Few passages in all the Bible state more pointedly the true source of prophetic power and the ultimate dependence of authentic religious experience upon the Lord. No person of himself or herself can speak of God; the message must come from God himself. Ancient prophets, apostles, reformers of the church such as Luther—all are alike. Not only is their word of proclamation one that comes from God, but they feel compelled to declare it.

When others seek to manipulate the Lord's word or to exploit divine powers as did Balaak, believers are challenged both to do what God bids and to speak what God says. No one should pretend that it is easy to know what God wants or to understand what he says. But all whose lives are bound in faith to him seek that divine will and listen for that divine word.

Hearing the Lord's Word (22:41 to 24:25)

Although Balaam had been engaged to curse Israel, he could not do so because God's word for Israel was one of blessing, not of cursing. On four successive occasions, Balaam blessed Israel, turning to various aspects of her heritage, her present, and her future. For those who will listen, God's word still comes across the ages to generate blessing for persons committed in faith through covenant relationships.

God's word of promise (22:41 to 23:12).—Ancient diviners often sought a sign from the gods by examining the vital organs of sacrificial animals. In this instance the offering of the seven sacrifices appear to have been for the purpose of eliciting an oracle from the Lord (cf. 23:3). Later, however, the text does state that Balaam made use of omens, physical evidences or witnesses to God's will (24:1).

The seven altars, with seven bulls and seven rams, suggest the com-

pleteness symbolized by the number seven, which originated from
the sun, the moon, and the five planets known to ancient persons.
In response, the Lord put a word in Balaam's mouth (v. 5) which
he was to share with Balak. Yet far from cursing Israel, Balaam could
only bless them. Fidelity to the Lord's word often sets one in conflict
with contemporary expectations, as it did in the case of Balaam and
Balak.

The word which came to Balaam focused on a vast people, dwelling
alone in the midst of the land (v. 9). Here we are reminded of the
multitude envisioned in the promise made to Abraham (cf. Gen. 12:2).
So Balaam's first oracle was intrinsically related to the theme of promise and fulfillment which so characterized Israel's life prior to the
conquest. What God promised to the patriarchs, he would fulfill
through the invasion under Moses and Joshua. Balaam's prophecy
underscored God's fidelity to the promises which flowed out of covenant relationships. God's word is a word of promise.

God's word of faithfulness (23:13-26).—Apparently convinced that
if the site of the sacrifices was changed to a place some distance from
the bulk of Israel, Balaam would not bless the invaders again, Balak
built seven more altars. Again the seven sacrifices were offered, and
again the Lord put a word in Balaam's mouth (v. 16). So the second
oracle was one of blessing rather than curse.

The central focus of the oracle stressed God's faithfulness: "God
is not man, that he should lie,/or a son of man, that he should repent./
Has he said, and will he not do it?" (v. 19). The promises God made
to the patriarchs were to be fulfilled. You can depend on the Lord
to fulfill the relationships which he sustains in the covenant. In response to Balaam's second blessing of Israel, Balak asked that he neither curse nor bless. Balaam's response showed his continuing commitment to the Lord and his message. It is on that quality of fidelity
by both God and persons that covenant relationships are maintained
in both ancient and modern societies.

God's word of fulfillment (23:27 to 24:13).—The unique aspect
of this third oracle is the fact that no longer did Balaam consult omens
(24:1). Rather, the Spirit of God came upon him to prompt the third
oracle. It consisted primarily of a portrait of Israel, presently encamped along the valleys stretching afar. God fulfilled what he promised earlier and more so: "Blessed be every one who blesses you,/
and cursed be every one who curses you" (v. 24:9). Those words appar-

ently are a direct appeal to God's promise to Abraham (Gen. 12:3). Angered by the threefold blessing which Balaam had extended to Israel, Balak told him that the promised honor was now forfeited. But in his retort Balaam reminded every believer that the prophetic word is not for sale (24:14).

God's word for the future (24:14-25).—The fourth oracle is actually integrated into Balaam's response to Balak following the third oracle. In the fourth oracle there are no sacrifices, no requests by Balak— only the solemn word of Balaam as a summation of the encounter with the Lord and the blessing of Israel.

Contrary to his previous insensitivity (cf. 22:21-34), Balaam made four self-affirmations: he was a person whose eyes were *open,* who heard the *words* of God, who knew the *knowledge* of God, and who saw the *vision* of the Almighty (vv. 15-16). In a prophetic oracle whose full reality did not come until a child was born in Bethlehem, Balaam saw the future purposes of God fulfilled for Israel in one from Jacob coming like a rising star, whose scepter would crush Moab. Perhaps Old Testament writers and theologians saw this fulfilled in David, and it may refer to those conquests of Moab by David. But that historical episode hardly exhausted the larger dimension of the oracle's theological significance. His coming was veiled in mystery, as Balaam said: "I see him, but not now/. . . a star shall come forth out of Jacob,/ and a scepter shall rise out of Israel;/it shall crush the forehead of Moab,/and break down the sons of Sheth" (v. 17). This was God's word for the future.

Preparing for a New Life (25:1 to 31:54)

Encamped across the Jordan from Jericho, Israel anticipated the movement across the river into the Promised Land. A variety of experiences on the plains of Moab are recorded by the compiler of the biblical material to illustrate the equipping of Israel for life in a new land. The experiences were recorded in retrospect and therefore show life in Moab from the perspective of later times. But there Israel confronted the lure of other gods (25:1-17), self-identity as God's people (26:1-65), sharing the inheritance (27:1-11), naming a successor to Moses (27:12-23), goodness of God (28:1 to 29:40), vowing oneself to God (30:1-16), and waging a holy war (31:1-54).

The Lure of Other Gods: Baal of Peor (25:1-18)

The lure of other gods which plagued Israel for all her history and which still plagues humanity was epitomized in the experience at Shittim. There Israel linked herself to Baal of Peor (v. 3). "Ba'al" means lord in the sense of owner and came to be applied to the god of the land. Those who worshiped Baal through the fertility rites of his shrines believed that such rites brought greater productivity to flock and herd, field and vineyard. Baal was the deity of settled, agrarian ways, and it raised a question that plagued Israel throughout her history. It is still a basic question for twentieth-century persons. Is the God and Father of our Lord Jesus Christ adequate for new situations and new cultures, or is he to be abandoned for the gods of a new era? Before Israel confronted the brunt of Canaanite Baalism, the issue was confronted and theoretically settled on the plains of Moab. Preparing for a new life involved dedicating oneself to the Lord, and Israel did it with a renewed affirmation of covenant faith.

The Second Census of God's People (26:1-65)

The second census of Israel took place on the plains of Moab, as recounted in chapter 26. As in the case of the first census (cf. Num. 1—4), a fundamental purpose of this one was to affirm that those included in the census were people of God. It was an exercise in identity, of identifying the people of God. Preparing to live a new life in Canaan involved a clear perception of their identity as people of God. To whom did they belong—by tribes, clans, and families? The answer was clear. They were the people of God, bound in covenant faith and relationship to the Lord as sovereign master of the covenant. So for all persons, no one can anticipate a new quality of life apart from a renewed awareness of one's identity in relationship with the Lord.

Sharing the Promised Inheritance (27:1-11)

A simple incident out of Israel's history led to the establishment of an operating principle in Israel. An Israelite named Zelophehad died with no sons but with five daughters. In an era when women did not normally inherit property, the question was appropriate: Why should the inheritance pass from the family? Thus, laws of inheritance were established which assured that family property should not pass to others (vv. 8-11). By so establishing this principle, an effort was made to guarantee the perpetuity of one's landed inheritance. Life and land were bound together in ancient Israel in ways that would appear strange to modern persons. But for Israel, preparing for a new life involved consideration for the land.

Naming a Successor to Moses (27:12-23)

Since Moses was denied access to the new land, it was necessary that his successor be chosen; and Joshua was picked for that task. Shared responsibility as a principle of leadership in Israel had been operative since Sinai. In the present instance Moses invested Joshua with a part of his authority so that he might begin to exercise leadership in the transition between the time of his investiture and the entrance into the land. Preparing for a new life in a new land required stable transition between changing leadership roles, together with the effort to maintain as leader one whose response to the Lord had been exemplary.

Celebrating God's Goodness (28:1 to 29:40)

These chapters constitute a calendar of annual sacrifices and special religious celebrations, giving parallel information much like that which appears in passages such as Exodus 12 and Leviticus 23. Among those celebrations were the daily offering (28:3-8), the sabbath offering (28:9-10), the monthly or new moon offering (28:11-15), the Feast of Unleavened Bread (28:16-25), the Feast of Weeks (28:26-31), the seventh month or New Year (29:1-6), the Day of Atonement (29:7-11), and the Feast of Tabernacles (29:12-38; cf. Lev. 23:33-36).

Although the offerings need not be discussed in detail, we can note that they uniquely emphasized the remembrance of God's goodness through his action in history. At times such remembrance focused on the redemptive experience out of Egypt. On other occasions persons remembered the wilderness, as in the Feast of Tabernacles. Or, again, they remembered the goodness of God through gifts of the land. But whatever the occasion, worship enabled Israel to remember the goodness of God in her history while reaffirming the reality of God's presence in both the present moments of worship and in life beyond the worship center. So worship recreated the past event of God in the present moment of worship while bringing to reality the power of God in the present moment of human experience. Before entering a new life in a new land, Israel affirmed a pattern for celebrating the joy of God's salvation.

Vowing Oneself to God (30:1-16)

Making a vow or a pledge to God was of utmost importance for ancient Israel, and vows could not be retracted arbitrarily. What one promised to do in his relationship with God, he must do. This was set forth clearly for Israel (vv. 1-2) with the only exceptions being the case of women whose vows were subject either to affirmation or rejection by fathers or husbands (vv. 3-15). A woman could make a vow, but she was treated as a minor because the fulfillment of the vow depended upon the response of the male figure, whether husband or father. For example, a woman could make a vow; but it was subject to the concurrence of her father (vv. 3-5) or her husband (vv. 6-8). Even the vows of widows or divorced women were conditioned by the prior attitude of husbands to those vows (v. 9). One restriction on the male's rights did emerge. He could nullify the vow on the day of first hearing about it, but he could not later rescind the vow.

While such restrictions are hardly consistent with the contemporary role of woman in modern society, they do reveal the absolute seriousness with which ancient Israel respected commitments made to God. Life in a new land involved keeping their vows to God.

Waging a Holy War (31:1-54)

To characterize war as "holy" runs so counter to contemporary understandings of the nature of war and biblical faith that we may forget that "holy wars" are as ancient as Israel of the conquest era. Neither is the Christian church without its history of wars waged against the so-called "heathen"; whether in the Crusades or in more recent centuries, such wars are indelibly inscribed on the pages of church history. This is not to justify war in the name of God, but it is to set the so-called primitive attitude of the Old Testament in proper perspective.

This present narrative of the battle with the Midianites reflects the same essential characteristics which we encounter later in the conquest era. First, the enemy was conquered in battle, warriors and kings were slaughtered, and the cities were burned, all in response to the command "to execute vengeance" (v. 3). The Lord was interpreted as the "lord of Hosts" who led the warriors, and enemy persons

as well as property were exterminated as a sacrifice of dedication.
Even the women captives, except the young girls, were killed at the
command of Moses when the warriors returned to the camp (vv.
14-18). The plunder from the raid was purified by fire or by water
(vv. 20-24). Then the booty was distributed between the warriors
and the congregation, with an appropriate "levy for the LORD."

How is one to understand such pillaging in the name of the Lord?
Consider one of two propositions: Either the nature and character
of God has changed, or the interpretation of holy war as the will of
God reflected the passing cultural concepts of the era rather than
the ultimate revelation of God. Has God changed, or has humanity's
understanding of God changed through the centuries? The latter
seems to be the case.

But in recognizing the temporary and conditional nature of Israel's
apprehension of God as expressed through holy war in the conquest
era, one should not overlook positive elements of Israel's commitment,
however much they may have reflected current cultural practices
of that era. For example, although holy war would not be justified
on the basis of the nature and character of God, reflected in that
practice is the affirmation of the Lord's uniqueness. For Israel there
was no other God. One sees also the conviction of destiny within
history. Each of these qualities is positive; but even so, they must
be held in check by the larger understanding of the nature and character of God. Left to run their own course apart from our larger understanding of the nature of God, those qualities can still lead us to a
dogmatic and despotic expression of faith which reflects more of the
holy war mentality than of the Spirit of God in Jesus Christ. But
despite contemporary Christian understandings, it is significant that
in being prepared for a new life in a new land, Israel was introduced
to the concept of holy war on the plains of Moab.

Living in a New Land (32:1 to 36:13)

As Israel anticipated the new land from east of the Jordan, seven
themes characterized that experience: anticipating the future (32:1-
42), remembering the journey (33:1-49), preparing for the crossing
(33:50-56), dividing the land (34:1-29), providing for the ministry (35:1-

8), protecting the innocent (35:9-34), and preserving the land (36:1-13). These individual themes probably emerged over a long period of time, however, and represent an idealized view of the sojourn. Probably several of the themes emerged after Israel faced particular problems during the settlement and following; but they were set in the context of Moab because of their consistency with the traditional roles and events associated with Moses. Whatever the history of their literary development, they constitute appropriate concerns which characterized the memory of Israel concerning her beginnings.

Anticipating the Future (32:1-42)

Two of the tribes, Reuben and Gad, decided that because of their occupations as cattle breeders, they preferred to settle the region of Gilead to the north of Moab. They did occupy that land, and the present narrative was included at this juncture in the book to explain the background of that fact. But when Moses responded to their request, he accused them of bringing about the same misfortune that befell Israel at Kadesh. Their remaining on the east side of the Jordan might discourage the people from entering the land just as the negative report of the spies had discouraged early Israel from entering the land immediately (vv. 6-15) Gad and Reuben proposed two conditions which won Moses' approval. First, they would go over and fight with the other tribes to secure the west bank of Jordan, leaving their families and cattle behind. Second, they would claim no part of the inheritance among those who settled on the west bank, since their inheritance had already been awarded on the east bank.

Thus, the sons of Gad and of Reuben, together with the half tribe of Manasseh, settled in the territory of the Amorites and the king of Bashan (vv. 33-42). This area became well known for its pastures and fat cattle, and later Old Testament references substantiated the settlement of cattle-raising Israelites in the area of Bashan. For example, Psalm 22 refers to this: "Many bulls encompass me,/strong bulls of Bashan surround me" (v. 12). Contrary to their ancestor Esau who had sold his birthright for a mess of pottage, forfeiting the future for present expediency, Reuben and Gad pledged their lives and families to the present conflict in order to secure the future. Anticipating the fulfillment of God's promises, persons of faith find the courage necessary to sacrifice today for a greater tomorrow.

Remembering the Journey (33:1-49)

To this date Israel has never forgotten the Exodus, the journey through the wilderness, and the conquest and settlement of the land. Those experiences are indelibly inscribed on their national consciousness, just as they are embodied in their worship experiences. Living in a new land demands that one remember the journey that one made in reaching the fulfillment of God's good promises. The fifty-eight place names mentioned in this chapter are significant because of their collective witness to the grace and mercy of God, who led Israel through such a varied and trying itinerary. Some of these names had little meaning to the Israel that prepared to enter Canaan, but in God's providence there are no common places. For the presence of God has the strangest way of making holy places out of common places. In many of these places the people had been blessed by God's grace and mercy that preserved life in the face of great difficulties. Israel never forgot whence she had come; nor should any generation. For our heritage consists of those common places made holy by the presence of God and hallowed by a depth of divine experience shared at those strange places. When people forget whence they have come, they usually forget where they are going, for the two are coupled together. Preparing to live in a new land involved remembering the past and its hallowed experiences at many common places.

Preparing for the Crossing (33:50-56)

As the people prepared to cross the Jordan and occupy the land, three dimensions characterized the Lord's counsel. First, in terms similar to the holy war, Israel was commanded to drive out the inhabitants and to destroy their religious objects as well as their worship centers. Second, they were to divide the land by lot and assign it in relation to the size of the tribes. Third, they were to drive out the inhabitants lest they remain to plague the Israelites "as pricks in your eyes and thorns in your sides" (v. 55).

Dividing the Land (34:1-29)

The boundaries of the land were established to the south (vv. 1-5), the west (v. 6), the north (vv. 7-9), and the east (vv. 10-12). These boundaries reflect the extent of the kingdom under David, and only in his time did the conquest go this far. But having described the four boundaries of the land, Moses commanded the people to divide the land among the nine tribes plus the half tribe of Manasseh (v. 13); the tribes of Reuben and Gad plus the other half of Manasseh were already assigned east of the Jordan. The chapter closes with a list of the leaders by tribes who were to receive the inheritance for division among the tribes.

Providing for the Ministry (35:1-8)

In dividing the land, appropriate measures were taken to provide for the ministry. Since the Levites were cared for through portions of the gifts and offerings carried to the shrine, they had no territory assigned within the land. They did, however, have forty-eight cities assigned to them, together with pasture lands extending two thousand cubits in each direction from the city.

Protecting the Innocent (35:9-34)

Regulations concerning the division of the land and the provisions made for the Levites automatically surfaced the issue of the six "cities of refuge," for those were occupied by the Levites. Those cities were established to protect the innocent person who killed another unintentionally (vv. 10-11). The "avenger" (v. 12) refers to the nearest of kin who was obliged by the ancient law of blood revenge to take the life of the person who killed his kinsman, however the death may have occurred. The cities of refuge, three on one side of Jordan and three on the other (vv. 14-15), assured that a person could not be killed until "he stands before the congregation for judgment" (v. 12). Their intent was to preclude irrational judgment, and it should be noted that one was protected from the avenger only until such time as the accused received an appropriate hearing.

Verses 16-21 list the kinds of murder in which revenge was justified, but verses 22-23 include instances of what today might be termed manslaughter and second- or third-degree murder. In those instances the slayer was safe in the city of refuge. Should he venture outside the city prior to the death of the high priest, however, the avenger might slay him with impunity (vv. 27-28). Additional precautions to protect human life involved the requirement that at least two witnesses were required in the case of a death penalty (v. 28). Also, it was impossible to ransom the life of a guilty person who fled to the city of refuge; apparently he was handed over to the avenger (v.

33). So, although primitive in origin, these ancient practices sought to assure that the innocent were protected—more so that taking human life should not be allowed to pollute the land by being unavenged. So in ancient Israel the rights of both the criminal and the assaulted person were maintained.

Preserving the Land (36:1-13)

Life and land were bound in unique ways for the ancient Israelite; indeed, in ways that are difficult for persons living in metropolitan areas to understand today. But for those reared in small towns or on farms there is a sense of loss in a person's separation from the land or from property. I remember, for example, that sense of loss when returning for the first of several visits with my parents who had sold the farm and other interests when they retired. There is a rootlessness without land and property for those who have held it.

To avert the passing of the land, Israel adopted the principle that "no inheritance shall be transferred from one tribe to another" (v. 9). The origin of this practice arose with the daughters of Zelophehad. Earlier the narratives suggested that they could inherit property since their father died with no male heirs (cf. 27:1-23). Now the issue emerged from another perspective. In the year of jubilee a woman's property normally would be joined to the tribe of her husband (v. 4). To avoid the loss of the land the daughters, and probably the daughters of other families and tribes, were commanded to marry only within their tribe. In this manner the land could not be passed to another tribe at the time of the year of jubilee (vv. 5-9). Consequently the daughters married into families of the sons of Manasseh, the son of Joseph.

In summary, as Israel prepared to enter the new land, they gave primary attention to anticipating the future, remembering the journey, preparing for the crossing, dividing the land, providing for the ministry, protecting the innocent, and preserving the land.

DEUTERONOMY

Introduction

Deuteronomy is a book of covenant relationships and demands in which the acts of God form the foundation of the author's appeal for Israel's decision. The covenant had already been made at Sinai, as reflected in Exodus 19—24. This recapitulation on the plains of Moab was to challenge later generations to commit life and energy to embodying the demands of covenant relationships.

Title

The English title "Deuteronomy" goes back to the Septuagint, the Greek translation of the Hebrew Old Testament. Although the title suggests "second law," that arises from a misunderstanding of how Deuteronomy 17:18 should be translated. Instead of "repetition of the law," it should be "copy" or "duplicate." Yet the title is suggestive of the content, for in Deuteronomy there is a "second giving" of the Law. In the Hebrew Bible the book's title came from its opening words: "These are the words"—that is, the words Moses spoke to all Israel.

Purpose

The book of Deuteronomy is a book of reformation, calling to renewal the members of the covenant community living long after the covenant originated. Although set on the plains of Moab during the closing days of Moses' life, before the conquest of the land, the book probably reached its full composition during a reform movement like that of Josiah late in the seventh century B.C. Its purpose was to call Israel to hear again the words of God and to make a new commitment to him. The book is characterized by exhortation or preaching, appealing to all who believe the covenant to live by its stipulations. It might be appropriately subtitled "The Preaching of the Covenant."

Characteristics

First, Deuteronomy has a strongly homiletical character. The author of the book did not merely collect or repeat a series of laws; he expounded them. He developed them with reference to the moral purposes which they serve.

Second, Deuteronomy reveals a lofty monotheism: "Hear, O Israel: the LORD our God is one LORD" (Deut. 6:4). Despite passages which refer to other deities subordinate to the Lord (cf. 13:2,6,13; 18:20; 12:2; 17:3), the central focus of the book is that of the singularity of God.

Third, love is a central element of God's nature, and the author saw evidences of that love in the history of Israel. It was through undeserved love that he brought them out of Egypt (8:3), and it was that love which sustained Israel. Love was also a primary characteristic of those in covenant with the Lord, and one to be emulated in succeeding generations (cf. 30:20 et al.)

Fourth, Deuteronomy linked ethical conduct with covenant life. The Lord was against filial impiety (5:6; 27:16; 21:18), murder (5:17), adultery (5:18), theft (5:19), dishonesty (25:13), false witness (5:20; 19:15 ff.). Lost animals were to be returned to their rightful owners (22:1 ff.), and a fellow Israelite was to be charged no interest for a loan (23:19).

Fifth, Deuteronomy demonstrates a spirit of reformation. Its purpose is to take the old laws and traditions and so impress them upon the people as to gain their commitment.

In summary, Deuteronomy acknowledges the Lord as the unique God of Israel, affirms his love, and insists that an appropriate response to the Lord is one of loving obedience. It teaches that the people of God are a holy people and are to manifest that quality of relationship by the way they live in all their relationships. Because the Lord is God, Deuteronomy insists that human life shall be just and generous and affirms the family and the teaching ministry of the home if persons are to recapitulate the faith of Sinai.

Preface (1:1-5)

The editoral introduction of the book is stated in the third person and introduces the book as "the words that Moses spoke to all Israel beyond the Jordan in the wilderness." The writer probably lived on the west bank and wrote later than the time of Moses. In fact, he found it necessary to remind those of his own day that it was an "eleven days' " journey from Horeb [Sinai] . . . to Kadesh-barnea" (v. 2), information readily available to those who made the original pilgrimage. But those addressed in the book probably lived after the time of Moses.

As in other books preceding Deuteronomy, the basis for Moses' speech was grounded in "all that the LORD had given him." He spoke the word of God directly, and the validity of his message was grounded not in himself but in the reality of God. It was beyond the Jordan in the land of Moab that Moses "undertook to explain this law"— that is, to interpret covenant stipulations and demands for the life of the covenant people. Moses' task as teacher/preacher is an ideal model for any age. He discovered the reality and the authority of what he said in the self-disclosure of God. And he gave himself to the ministry of assisting others to understand with him the implications of God's revelation for life.

The Deeds and the Demands of God
1:6 to 4:40

The confessional and hortatory nature of Deuteronomy is clearly reflected in the three speeches of Moses and is equally implicit in the other two major parts of Deuteronomy. For example, in the first speech of Moses there is a finely balanced emphasis between the deeds of God (chaps. 1—3) and the demands of God (chap. 4). In Moses' second speech (chaps. 5—11) there follows a comparable contrast between the nature of God (chap. 5) and the demands that flow from his character (chaps. 6—11). The third speech (chaps. 29—30) continues that balanced appeal for persons to respond to the Lord. Also, Deuteronomy 29:1-17, much like chapters 1 and 3 is essentially a confession of the mighty acts of God. The remainder of the address (29:18 to 30:20) is an eloquent pleading for Israel to respond positively in her moment of decision; she faces "life and good, death and evil" (30:15) between which she is obliged to choose. In all of the addresses of Moses there is the principle of confession and exhortation: confession of what God has done and who God is, plus an appeal to Israel that she might respond worthily to the Lord's self-revelation in history.

Proclaiming God's Mighty Acts (1:6 to 3:29)

These chapters constitute a resumé of God's mighty acts during Israel's pilgrimage between Sinai and Moab. Throughout Deuteronomy "Horeb" is used as a synonym for "Sinai"; but because of the greater familiarity of most persons with Sinai, that usage will have priority here rather than Horeb. The deeds of God and the response of Israel may be summarized well in these chapters as a portrait in fear and in failure (1:6-46) and as a portrait in providential leadership (chaps. 2—3).

A Portrait in Fear and in Failure (1:6-46)

Challenged to leave the security of Sinai where the Lord had so gloriously manifested himself, Israel was prompted to leave that mountain scene (vv. 6-8), cooperate in achieving God's purposes (vv. 9-

18), and conquer the land God had promised so long before to Abraham (vv. 19-46). Confronted by that challenge, Israel's response was a portrait, in both fear and failure, of a people whose fears so eroded their commitment as to assure their failure. Such a study is appropriate for all today who confront in modern society the polarities of fear and failure.

The call to commitment (1:6-8).—God's call to commitment resounds to arouse all covenant people who have grown content with the security of familiar surroundings and the assured presence of God. With Israel, those who grow self-satisfied in the comfortable familiarity of the church should hear the Lord: "You have stayed long enough at this mountain" (v. 6). The challenge is sure, comprehensive, and clear: "Turn and take your journey" (v. 7). People of God are a pilgrim people, always on the way to achieving the unfulfilled purposes of God's tomorrows. This is the call to commitment for the church of all ages: You've stayed long enough where you are; be on your journey as befits a pilgrim people.

The call to cooperation (1:9-18).— The principle of shared leadership emerges again here in the choice of the seventy elders of Israel as it had in the book of Exodus and Numbers (Ex. 18:13 ff.; Num. 11:10-17). Each narrative includes aspects not in the other two, but in all three there is a unified witness to the concept of sharing responsibilities. The success of Israel as a covenant community, as of the new covenant, demanded the implementation of that principle. God's call to conquest is a call to cooperation.

The call to conquest (1:19-46).—God's call to Israel set in motion twin polarities: fear of God and fear of persons. Although deeply aware of the fear of God born at Sinai, that aweful experience was displaced at Kadesh-barnea by the fear of the Canaanites and what might happen should Israel invade the land. The abortive effort to gain the land at Kadesh may be seen from four perspectives.

First, the goodness of God's goal was apparent in 1:19-25: "It is a good land which the LORD our God gives us" (v. 25). The expedition by the twelve spies to survey the land (Num. 13—14) reappears here in abbreviated form. The question was not the goodness of the land (v. 25), but the commitment of Israel to the purpose of God in the face of what seemed to be overwhelming obstacles.

Second, there are times *when the faithful falter* (1:26-33). The reason Israel faltered at the prospect of achieving the Lord's promise is not difficult to discover: "Yet you would not go up . . . you did not believe the LORD your God" (vv. 26,32). To believe God is to trust him and to act in the context of that trust, no matter what the comparative size and power of one's opposition. It was not that the goal was questionable, but the lack of disciplined commitment necessary for its achievement that led to the failure at Kadesh. The same remains forever true. It is neither the value nor the goodness of the goal; all agree on that. It is the price demanded to achieve that goal that produces both fear and failure. The portraits of fear and failure are essentially the same in all generations. Only the almost indistinguishable touches of the artist or the coloration on life's canvas betrays the differences between one era and another.

Third, Israel's failure lay in *forfeiting the future* (1:34-40). To succumb to the fear of persons rather than to commit oneself to the fear of God leads a person to forfeit the future: "Not one of these . . . shall see the good land" (v. 35). Only two categories of persons lived to see the goodness of the land: those spies who brought positive reports, Caleb and Joshua; plus those children about whom the elders had been so concerned when they turned back at Kadesh (v. 39). All others forfeited the future—even Moses and Aaron, although for entirely different reasons. To succumb to fear is to forfeit one's claim to the future.

Fourth, Israel's tardy response to the Lord's challenge is illustrative of the danger of *learning too late* (1:41-46). After hearing the Lord's reprimand, the people may have made an abortive attempt to enter the land. Aware of their failure, the people repented: "We have sinned against the LORD; we will go up and fight" (v. 41). But it was too late. The opportunity had slipped through their fingers. Hear the Lord's counsel through Moses: "Do not go up or fight, for I am not in the midst of you" (v. 42). But Israel was determined and sought to go up into the hill country, despite the Lord's caution. But "the Amorites who lived in that hill country came out against [them] and chased [them] as bees" (v. 44). So Israel "returned and wept before the LORD; but the LORD did not hearken" (v. 45). They remained at Kadesh-barnea for a long stay (v. 46).

It is possible to learn from one's mistaken judgments and to correct one's life. But it is also possible to learn too late. It is too late when the unique confluence of time and circumstance has passed and the opportunity, once so laden with possibility, is no more. For most persons there is a single, unique, and distinctive opportunity. When it is gone, it is too late to learn. As with great athletes, timing is crucial to first-rate performance; to sense the time and to move at that precise moment is required to achieve the purpose of God. But the purposes of God are never fully achieved by persons who learn too late. Another generation or another person will fulfill that divine promise, but not the person who always learns too late.

A Portrait in Providential Leadership (2:1 to 3:29)

One generation fails the Lord, but another succeeds at the same challenge. On this rests the future of God's purposes: Someone somewhere will respond to a challenge which others thought impossible to dream, much less to achieve. So chapters 2 and 3 are a study in providential leadership as God led the battered Israelites across the wilderness, searching for the promise made to Abraham. God may give us up to our own rebellious ways, but he never gives up on us. That is humanity's hope. And that was the hope of Israel.

Command of God for a chastened people (2:1-3).—Turning back from Kadesh, Israel moved southeastward toward the Red Sea (the Gulf of Aqaba, and not to be confused with the sea Israel originally crossed). For many days they wandered, until the Lord sounded words so like those that called them to leave Sinai. Those words call to every battered, disconsolate person: "You have been going about this mountain country long enough; turn northward" (v. 3). "Northward" lay the Promised Land, and it was to that land that God was leading Israel. Chastened by their failure and anxious because of their travail, Israel responded to God's command that they not outlive their dream, that they keep in focus the area "northward" where the fulfillment of God's purposes lay. Whatever the chastening and however much the discouragement, the people of God are to keep moving "northward" toward the purposes of God.

Consideration for God's purposes (2:4-23).—In pursuing their pilgrimage northward toward the land God promised, Israel was cautioned to respect God's promises to Esau and Lot. The Edomites who lived in Seir (v. 4) were descendants of Esau with whom the Lord had dealt graciously, even as with Jacob (v. 5). "So we went on, away from our brethren the sons of Esau who live in Seir, away from the Arabah road from Elath and Eziongeber" (v. 8).

Neither was Israel permitted to encroach on the land of Moab, for that land had been given to "the sons of Lot for a possession" (v. 9). The writer also explains how Esau had dispossessed the Horites (also called Emim or Rephaim) and taken Seir for himself and his people (vv. 10-12).

Israel was commanded to follow the deep valley where the brook Zered ran its course into the southeast end of the Dead Sea. The Zered was the dividing line of Edom and Moab (vv. 13-14). A short note of explanation tells of the death of all those God had said would not enter the Promised Land (v. 14). The "hand of the Lord" was usually used in reference to helping Israel. In verse 15 the phrase is used of God turning on the Israelites that were not to enter Canaan.

As the Israelites began making their way toward entering Canaan, they were warned not to bother the land of the Ammonites. God had promised this land as a possession of the sons of Lot (v. 19).

Although the narrative has as its central focus for a later generation the explanation that Israel did not conquer these areas, there is also a larger purpose. The narrative emphasizes the Lord's fidelity to promises made in the context of Israel's long history, reaching back to the times of the patriarchs. God is faithful, and his purposes both for Israel and for others are dynamic factors in history.

Conquest of the noncooperative (2:24 to 3:11).—But what of those who had not shared in the old promises and who withstood the purposes of God during Israel's pilgrimage? Sihon, king of Heshbon, was conquered (2:24-37); and Og, king of Bashan, was overpowered (3:1-7). The summary of those conquests (3:8-11) reflects the practice of putting others to the ban—that is, dedicating them to the Lord through extermination. That aspect of holy war is uniquely suggested in the word translated "utterly destroyed" (v. 6). It is from a Hebrew word which is closely related to the idea of holiness. That which had belonged to another god was dedicated to the Lord by putting an end to persons, animals, and property. In keeping with the concept of holy war, the extermination of these nations was a religious act, however much that may run counter to contemporary Christian sensibilities. Admittedly, it was an ancient practice more closely related to culture than to the ultimate expression of God's will; holy war was one facet of Israel's pilgrimage in apprehending the nature and character of God. Influenced by cultural practices of the era, Israel interpreted the holy war as an expression of God's purpose.

Consolidation and extension of territory (3:12-22).—Following the conquest of areas east of the Jordan, Israel divided that territory and planned the extension of the campaign to the west bank of Jordan. First, the conquered territory was distributed to Gad and Reuben (vv. 12-17). Second, Gad and Reuben were to continue to aid their brethren in conquering the western territory (vv. 18-21). Third, Joshua was encouraged for the west bank campaign; and although there is no specific designation of him as successor of Moses, the text implies as much (v. 22; cf. Num. 27:12-23).

Condemnation of Moses (3:23-29).—Moses was condemned to view from Mount Pisgah a land that he could never enter (vv. 23-29). Though he sought the Lord's favor in requesting that he be permitted to "go over, I pray, and see the good land" (v. 25), his prayer was denied. Dying in Moab, Moses, like so many, forfeited the future through presuming on the grace and power of God (cf. Num. 27:12-14; Deut. 32:48-52).

Remembering What God Has Done (4:1-40)

Having proclaimed the mighty acts of God (chaps. 1—3), Moses challenged Israel to remember and to act in the context of God's gracious actions. The chapter is an urgent and moving appeal directed to the memory of Israel. As all succeeding covenant persons, she was to keep the law because of the greatness of God's revelation. Because of what God had done, Israel was urged to remember the deeds of God (4:1-8), the revelation of God (4:9-24), the alternatives of God (4:25-31), and the uniqueness of God (4:32-40).

Remembering the Deeds of God (4:1-8)

The chapter begins "And now" (v. 1), as though to say, seeing what God has done (chaps. 1—3), "give heed" (v. 1) to the revelation of God. In remembering the deeds of God at Baal-peor (v. 3; Num. 27:12 ff.) and the revelation which God shared (vv. 5-6), three elements are primary: the action of God (vv. 1-4), the knowledge of God (vv. 5-6), and the presence of God (vv. 7-8).

The action of God (4:1-4).—An adequacy associated with God's action in revelation found expression in the exhortation: "You shall not add to the word which I command you, nor take from it" (v. 2).

The Word is adequate. For those who might question this, God's action in dealing with both faithless and faithful persons should be instructive. The fate of the faithless at Baal-peor was clear: "Your eyes have seen . . . for the LORD your God destroyed . . . all the men who followed the Baal" (v. 3). But the fate of the faithful is equally instructive: "but you who held fast to the LORD your God are all alive this day" (v. 4).

The knowledge of God (4:5-6).—Faithful teaching had been shared by Moses, who taught what the Lord had commanded. God's action through Moses precipitated knowledge of God among the people. Taught by God, Moses taught others (v. 5). Such knowledge of God, experiential and dynamic in personal lives, will bring about three things in a believer's life. He will *keep* what God teaches, *do* what God teaches, and *discover* both "your wisdom and your understanding in the sight of the peoples" (v. 6).

The presence of God (4:7-8).—Life's greatest gift is oneself; and God gave himself, not just truth about himself. The concept of the presence of God permeated the whole of Israel's experience from the Exodus forward. Even in the call of Moses the concept of presence was primary. So in corporate Israel: "For what great nation is there that has a god so near to it as the LORD our God is to us" (v. 7). Second only to the presence of God was the reality of the law, which was given not as a penal burden to be borne but as a light to guide Israel in fulfilling covenant relationships.

Remembering the Revelation of God (4:9-24)

The second exhortation in Moses' sermon to Israel focused on remembering the revelation of God. Someone has said that the fourth chapter of Deuteronomy is a commentary on the second commandment: "You shall have no other gods before me" (Deut. 5:7). Why is this so? Because God revealed himself not through the rigid form of an idol but through a dynamic and creative Word. God was revealed to Israel at Sinai not by images but by words and deeds of redemption.

Revelation and remembrance are inseparable (4:9).—The people of God are not only to remember the revelation of God, lest they forget what they have experienced; they are to share this with their children and their children's children (v. 9). Such an emphasis on teaching and learning is consistent with other emphases on teaching within Deuteronomy. Also, the words "remember" and "forget" involve far more than the elemental issue of forgetfulness or lapse of memory, or the sudden act of remembering something which had slipped from memory. Rather, the words suggest deliberate acts of repudiation on the one hand (forget) and times of serious commitment/recommitment on the other. One is to guard or treasure one's experience with the Lord. An element of nurture is involved in maintaining a person's relationships.

Revelation and word are inseparable (4:10-14).—The word as revelation may be either audible or inaudible. As Psalm 19:3-4 says, "There is no speech, nor are there words . . . yet their voice goes out through all the earth/and their words to the end of the world." Israel saw no form at Sinai; they heard a voice (v. 12). Such a word of revelation must be *communicated* to people, *appropriated* through personal reverential awe or "fear," and *transmitted* or taught to one's children—although the Word is a dynamic quality that can be neither taught nor learned in the sense that ultimately it can only be experienced for oneself (v. 10).

Revelation and idolatry are incompatible (4:15-24).—Idolatry was rejected in Israel because it represented an effort to objectify God, reducing him to a single aspect of his revelation. Revelation comes through the Word: living, active, and dynamic. At times that word is like new wine, fermenting and active, churning in the heat of its own movement—unable to rest in old wineskins, to use Jesus' analogy.

Contemporary forms of idolatry are rampant though subtle. An understanding of God which presumes to limit God to a single aspect of his nature and character is a subtle form of idolatry. To state an extreme illustration, not even the church or the Bible should be substituted for God; they bear witness to him. Ultimately God comes to us in the dynamic reality of the Word: the creative, redeeming power of God in our lives to address the inner person in ways appropriate for the total person.

Remembering the Alternatives of God (4:25-31)

Deuteronomy often casts its message through the use of polarities. In addition to the polarities in the larger speeches in which God's action or character (cf. chaps. 1—3) are set against human response (chap. 4), other patterns also emerge. For example, the closing cycle of the book places cursing and blessing before the people (chap. 26) or the ways of life and death (30:15). So here also, the polar alternatives of God are clear: scattered among the nations (vv. 25-28) or searching for God (vv. 20-31).

Scattered among the nations (4:25-28).—In a passage reminiscent of her exilic period of history, Israel confronted the first alternative. Should they "act corruptly by making a graven image" (v. 25), God would utterly destroy Israel and scatter them among the nations (vv. 27-28). Those who abandon the dynamic reality of the word as the focus of relationship with God can anticipate no less than a comparable disintegration of relationship. Creative, meaningful relationships with him rise out of the creative power of word/event as the focus of identity with God.

Searching for God (4:29-31).—Should a people who have been scattered, as in the Exile of the sixth century B.C., seek the Lord, they will find him. But note the condition: "If you search after him with all your heart and with all your soul" (v. 29). This is the second alternative. God responds both positively and creatively to those who search with the wholeness of life: "For the LORD your God is a merciful God; he will not *fail* you or *destroy* you or *forget* the covenant" (v. 31, author's italics). Both the option and the fates belong to individuals: scattered from the Lord through broken relationships, or joined to the Lord through covenant mercy and fidelity.

Remembering the Uniqueness of God (4:32-40)

This exhortation to Israel, as to later covenant persons, closes with five unique characteristics of God in relationship to the covenant community, plus a final exhortation.

Unique in action (4:32).—What the Lord has done in history is unique. One may look at religions of the world and discover positive moral factors or exemplary human figures. But nowhere does one find a comparable emphasis on God's unique action in history as in biblical religion. The challenge is clear, Ask as far back in time as creation, or spatially "from one end of heaven to the other, whether such a great thing as this has ever happened or was ever heard of" (v. 32). God's action, then and today, is unique in history.

Unique in revelation (4:33).—In what way is God's action in history unique? His action is unique because he spoke to Israel (v. 33). Whether one understands the nature of "speaking" as external and audible or internal and inaudible, God is unique in revelation. Other gods are revealed through the rigid, fixed forms of idols. But God's revelation comes through living Word. It is the uniqueness of the Word of God that gives the biblical revelation a uniqueness ultimately manifested when "the Word became flesh and dwelt among us, full of grace and truth" (John 1:14).

Unique in redemption (4:34).—God is also unique in his redemptive activity. What other deity had acted to redeem persons as had the Lord? "Or has any god ever attempted to go and take a nation for himself from the midst of another nation?" (v. 34). Such reference to the uniqueness of the Exodus as a redemptive event could be extended to other acts of redemption in history—finding its ultimate fulfillment on a hill outside the city wall of Jerusalem, counterbalanced by an open tomb and a risen Redeemer. What other deity had acted in so unique a fashion to redeem humanity?

Unique in communion (4:35-36).—Two aspects of the communion generated through God's redemption are significant. First, God acted in so unique a fashion as he did in the Exodus event and at Sinai in order that "you might know that the LORD is God" (v. 35). Second, God shared himself with Israel through his word "that he might discipline you" (v. 36). The word "discipline" in biblical Hebrew is from a root word meaning to teach, take advice, listen to reason. From that usage the word "disciple" derives. Hence discipline is not limited to the negative connotation of punishment but also means teaching and learning. God gave himself to us that he might lead us in learning or discipleship.

Unique in devotion (4:37-40).—The Lord is also unique in his devotion to persons. It was because "he *loved* your fathers and *chose* their descendants" that he brought Israel out of Egypt (v. 37). Such devotion to the people and to the promises made to the patriarchs prompted the Lord to give the land as an inheritance (v. 38). In the context of such devotion, one should "know . . . [lay it to your heart] . . . there is no other" (v. 35). Christians often sing of that singular devotion: "No one ever cared for me like Jesus," for the Lord is unique in his devotion.

The latter part of the chapter is direct and forceful, challenging persons to respond to the Lord's uniqueness. "Therefore" (v. 40), because of who God is and what he has done, persons are challenged to live out of his revelation.

Cities of refuge (4:41-43).—These verses show a change of writing style. They compose an interlude or break in the writing of Deuteronomy. Chapter 19 deals more fully with the cities of refuge and their meaning. You may wish to turn to chapter 19 and read it at this point.

The Character of God and the Conduct of Man

4:44 to 11:32

The Ten Words (cf. Deut. 4:13), more commonly known as the Ten Commandments, appear in both Exodus 20 and Deuteronomy 5. They constitute the highly compressed stipulations attached to covenant relationships and convey the demand of God for redeemed persons. But viewed from another perspective, the Ten Words are also an index to the character of God. Just as legislation passed by a state or national legislature is an index to the character of elected officials, so the Ten Words portray the character of God. The polarity to God's character is the conduct of persons. For chapters 6—11 constitute a clearly delineated statement of what it means to be the people of God. Hence one might outline the second speech of Moses according to the character of God (chap. 5) and the conduct of man (chaps. 6—11).

The Giving of the Law (4:44-49)

But prior to the beginning of Moses' second speech, there is an introduction to the giving of the law. First, the law was described with regard both to its content (v. 44) and to the locale of its declaration (v. 46). The law consisted of the *testimonies*, the *statutes*, and the *ordinances*. While these three categories should not be interpreted as rigid distinctions, they did come from a late Old Testament era when the law had fully developed. Each word gives a careful distinction of categories within the larger law. Second, the law was ascribed to the time when Israel encamped to Moab, across the Jordan; and according to Deuteronomy, Moses gave the law a "second time." The giving of the law was also linked to the conquest of the trans-Jordan tribes (vv. 47-49).

The Character of God (5:1-33)

Who God is may be determined in part by what he demands from those bound with him in covenant. The same is true of religion generally, for its demands are an index to its character.

Revealing the Ten Words (5:1-21)

Command of God (5:1-5).—The content of God's command is clear: Hear, learn, and do all that God speaks (v. 1). For the covenant was not just with the fathers of those who stood on the plains of Moab, but with the persons themselves (vv. 2-4). The covenant was with the patriarchs, and the law was given at Sinai; but their pertinence is ever present. The important factor is not that the Lord made a covenant with someone else in the history of the synagogue or the church, but that you yourself have a covenant with the Lord: "The LORD spoke with you face to face" (v. 4). The consequence of that appearance is appropriate for every new meeting with the Lord: "for you were afraid" (v. 5). Despite the fact that love casts out certain qualities of fear, there remains a responsible emphasis on fear as reverential awe and response to the Lord which is appropriate for every generation of believers.

Confessional proclamation of the Lord's redemptive deed (5:6).— The foundations of the Commandments rest in God's redemptive action. They were and are addressed to redeemed persons, not to persons untouched and unmoved by God's redeeming grace. In Judaism such focus on the historical character of God's redemption is so significant that verse 6 is considered to be the First Commandment: "I am the LORD your God." Such a redemptive statement was confessional in that it arose from faith as opposed to rationally demonstrated proof. The Egyptians and the Hebrews likely differed greatly in their later reflections on the deliverance from Egypt. For Israel the event was interpreted from the stance of faith and so was a confessional statement on God's redeeming action.

Character of God revealed in the Ten Words (5:7-21).—Detailed examinations of the Commandments must be sought either in full-scale commentaries or in special works on the Ten Commandments, and only two major themes will be discussed in this treatment. (Individual commandments will be identified within parentheses by Roman numerals, followed by the verse reference.) The first four of the Ten Words stress *the worth and the worship of God* (vv. 7-15). The worth of God flows from his uniqueness; for covenant persons there is only one God (I; v. 7).

God as the only God for believers is to be worshiped in the appropriate manner; and revelation comes through the word, not through the static form of idols (II; vv. 8-10). As important as was the rejection of the idol in worship, so was the affirmation of the name as a symbol for the reality of God's presence in and through his name. So his name was not to be lifted up "for emptiness," for no good purpose (III; v. 11). By hallowing one day in seven, persons symbolically acknowledged that all time belongs to God, and thereby symbolically gave it to him (IV; vv. 12-15).

The concluding six Commandments focus on the theme that other persons have rights, too (vv. 16-21). The vertical and the horizontal dimensions of the Ten Words have often been emphasized—the vertical speaking directly to one's relationship to God, the horizontal focusing on interpersonal relationships with other covenant persons. While this can be unduly emphasized by excluding man from the first four Commandments and God from the concluding six Commandments, the primary emphasis is correct.

What are central rights which flow from covenant relationships? Parents have the right to anticipate respect from children, and that on the adult level (V; v. 16). Persons have the right to life in the fullest sense (VI; v. 17). Adultery is precluded within the covenant community, husbands having the right to assume that others will respect the fidelity of their marriage (note the male-oriented character of early Israel's stipulations (VIII; v. 18). Persons have the right to assume that individuals in the covenant community will respect their right to property (VIII; v. 19). There is the right to anticipate truth in human relationships—legal, social, individual, and corporate (IX; v. 20). Persons also have the right to be free from covetousness which eventuates in taking what does not rightly belong to the oppressor (X; v. 21).

Receiving the Ten Words (5:22-27)

How did Israel receive the Lord's revelation through the Ten Words? At least three aspects of that reception emerge within the text (vv. 22-27).

Sufficiency of the word (5:22).—The adequacy of the Ten Words seems clearly reflected in the statement that "he added no more" (v. 22). The Ten Words need to be reshaped and adapted to emerging, new situations; but in themselves they are adequate statements of fundamental principles to guide covenant living. Jesus, as one will recall, affirmed the validity of the Commandments; but in his use of them he went beyond their original application (cf. Matt. 5:17-32). The Commandments do not need to be expanded or superseded nearly so much as they need to be applied to the human situation. Some say that the Commandments "won't work" in a modern era, but neither does soap if it is not applied.

Speaking with God (5:23-27).—Undue familiarity with God can lead one to a superficiality which has no fear of God. But this was far from the case with ancient Israel. In speaking with God at the mountain they became keenly aware of their inability to know and to experience the immediacy of God's ultimate presence. *God's self-disclosure* came as they heard the voice out of the midst of darkness (vv. 23-24). The writer described three features of the experience: (1) they had seen God's glory and greatness; (2) they had heard his voice; (3) they had seen him and yet lived (v. 24).

Yet, despite such self-disclosure of God's person, there remained a *gulf between persons and God* (vv. 25-26). Israel acknowledged that they could not approach the fullness of God's glory and power. The need for a mediator became apparent, and it was to Moses that Israel turned, asking that he "Go near, and hear . . . and speak to us all that the LORD our God will speak to you" (v. 27). Covenant-mediator Moses traced a pattern for the mediatorial role later fulfilled by Jesus the Christ, who became for New Testament believers the only mediator between God and persons.

Submitting to God (5:27).—Israel's mood in responding to the Lord's revelation was a model of commitment: "The LORD our God will speak to you; and we will hear and do it" (v. 27). The double meaning of the Hebrew word focuses on both hearing and obeying. One has not heard in the biblical sense if he has not obeyed. So with the revelation of God in the personal and immediate sense, there has been no revelation if one makes no response. Revelation consists in the meeting of God and persons in personal interaction.

Responding to Human Reaction (5:28-33)

How does the Lord respond when persons commit themselves to him as Israel did?

Loyalty to revelation commended (5:28).—When the Lord spoke again to Moses, he commended the people: "They have rightly said all that they have spoken" (v. 28).

Longing for loyalty (5:29).—This exhortation may well reflect a time when Israel had forgotten the earlier commitment at Sinai and at Moab. But whatever its date of origin, the statement reflects a longing for constant fidelity: "Oh that they had such a mind as this always, to fear me and to keep all my commandments" (v. 29).

Legal expansion of the Ten Words (5:30-31).—The command to Moses that he remain with the Lord to receive "all the commandment and the statutes and the ordinances" (v. 31) is consistent with a view of the Ten Words which presupposes that they are the foundation on which all other stipulations were erected in Israel. The Ten Words, given as direct, unequivocal commandments, constituted the fountain-head from which all other stipulations flowed. As new situations were confronted, new applications of the Ten Words were made in the form of additions to the legal code(s).

Leaving the revelation of God (5:32-33a).—Turning neither to the right hand nor to the left (v. 32), Israel was prohibited from leaving the way which the Lord revealed. "You shall walk in all the way" (v. 33*a*).

Life as the consequence of faithfulness (5:33b).—Life is both God's gift and God's goal for persons. Biblical religion is consistently life-affirming, not life-denying, whether in the Old Testament or in the New Testament. Living in God's revelation is not only related to the good life now, but to the longevity of life: "That it may go well with you, and that you may live long in the land."

The Conduct of Man (6:1 to 11:32)

These six chapters focus on the conduct of persons bound in cove-nant with the Lord. In his book on Deuteronomy, Pythian-Adams astutely observed that these chapters may be viewed as a commentary on the First Commandment. If there is only one God, what are the implications of that belief for Israel or for succeeding believers in the church who affirm that the uniqueness of God logically presupposes a unique life-style for those committed to relationship with him? If there is one God and one God only, then there is one faithful fellowship (chap. 6), one people of God (chap. 7), one source of life (chap. 8), one source of success (chap. 9), one ultimate relationship (chap. 10), and one fundamental choice (chap. 11).

One God—One Faithful Fellowship (6:1-25)

If there is only one God, then it follows that there is a single fellowship of covenant persons bound in faith within the circle of commitment to that God.

A fearful fellowship (6:1-3).—"Fear" is the closest synonymn which biblical Hebrew has to the English word "religion." It suggests both the awe and the wonder associated with one's experience with God, together with an element of fear in the traditional connotation of that word. But it does not suggest terror, for which biblical Hebrew had a specific word. What is the purpose of the revelation of God, and what is the nature of the covenant community? The answer is clear: "That you may fear the Lord your God" (v. 2). The fate of this fellowship in the future will be determined largely by believers' faithfulness to the revelation, together with the propriety of the response which they make to God (vv. 2-3).

Fundamentals of the faith (6:4-9).—If there are many gods, then what one believes about any one of them is marginally significant. But if there is only one God, the fundamentals of the faith are exceedingly significant. *First, faith must be perceived* (vv. 4-5). These verses constitute the *Shema* (the first word, "Hear!") of Judaism, which embodies the crystallization of faith: (1) "The LORD our God is one LORD; and (2) you shall love the LORD your God with all your heart, and with all your soul, and with all your might." Do you see the polarities: the singularity of God as a polar concentration for faith, counterbalanced by love for him? This must be perceived clearly, for it is one of the primary fundamentals of the faith.

Second, faith must be practiced (6:6-9).—The words that summarize the fundamentals of faith are to be upon the heart—that is, the intellect or will (v. 6). They are to be taught to children (v. 7*a*), talked about, and lived out in life (v. 7*b*). Such words as constitute the fundamentals of faith are before one constantly; one never lives apart from them. The literal implementation of this command led to writing the Shema on the doorposts (v. 9) or printing the words so that they could be worn as "frontlets between your eyes" or bound as "a sign upon your hand" (v. 8). But the fundamental issue is not whether one literally reproduces the Shema in these fashions but whether one lives each day under its constant implications. However achieved, it is important that the fundamentals of the faith be practiced and kept ever before succeeding generations.

Third, the fundamentals of the faith must be perpetuated (6:4-9).—Teaching and learning are unique emphases of Deuteronomy, and especially does the Shema enjoin this responsibility upon the family: "You shall teach them diligently to your children" (v. 7). Faith is not only to be perpetuated in one's own life (vv. 4-6) but to be offered with equal vigor in the lives of others (vv. 7-9). The ministry of the teaching church will never reach its full potential apart from the home. Nor can the family attain its proper stability and moral influence apart from the role of the teaching church. Each is partner with the other in perpetuating the faith.

A forgotten father (6:10-15).—There can be no faithful fellowship of believers if persons forget God their Father, who made possible life in the new land. The goodness of that land was a reward for which Israel had not labored. They came into a land with cities which they had not built, houses full of good things which they had not filled; they drank from cisterns which they had not dug; and they ate from vineyards and olive groves that they had not planted (vv. 10-11). Lest they forget the Lord who made this possible, Moses reminded them to remember the Lord during their days of abundance (v. 12). More so, he challenged them positively by encouraging them to fear the Lord, to serve him, and to swear by his name (v. 13). Negatively he counseled them not to follow other gods, knowing "the LORD your God, is a jealous God" (v. 15). For every person the haunting words of Rudyard Kipling are still appropriate: "Lord God of Hosts, be with us yet, Lest we forget—lest we forget!"

Testing or trusting (6:16-19).—Again, the issues of life are set as polarities: Test God or trust God—which shall it be? Moses counseled against putting the Lord to the test as at Massah (v. 16). The same theme later emerged in Jesus' ministry: "You shall not tempt the Lord your God" (Luke 4:12). It remains a word of caution for all whose action would put God's patience to the test.

Contrary to testing God is the positive commitment to trust him. This ideal response pleases God by complete obedience through keeping the Commandments (v. 17), doing what is right and good (v. 18). Such conduct would lead to success in the conquest (vv. 18-19), for such conduct not only brings its own reward; God directly rewards fidelity.

The meaning of life and law (6:20-25).—The question-and-answer motif was used throughout the book of Deuteronomy and in other material influenced by Deuteronomy. The question is deliberately asked in order to permit a theological answer. The meaning of life is a constant issue for every generation. What's the meaning of it all—worship, ministry, service, mission?

The answer to the meaning of life may be discovered in the action of God (vv. 21-24). How was Israel to answer their sons in future generations? "Then you shall say to your son, 'We were Pharaoh's slaves in Egypt'" (v. 21). We are to tell our descendants what God has done in our lives, how his redemptive action invaded history to bring salvation (vv. 22-24). Modern persons can do no better than to tell their children what God has done, for in this they discover the ultimate meaning of life.

One God—One People (7:1-26)

The word "exclusivism" has an essentially negative connotation for many persons, but it is a legitimate implication of the belief in only one God. Although one has a measure of hesitation in speaking of the legitimacy of exclusivism, there is a unique quality of intolerance in biblical religion (vv. 1-5). For example, the defeat and all but disregard for pagan nations (vv. 1-3) reflects the command "You must utterly destroy them" (v. 2). Central to that purging of the land was the assumption that compromise leads to apostasy; therefore, avoid it (v. 4). Because of these attitudes non-Israelite religious structures were exterminated as one facet of the holy war which attended the conquest of Canaan (v. 5).

Whether exclusivism is an appropriate response to contemporary world religions today must be determined against the background of the Bible's affirmation of the uniqueness of biblical revelation. For biblical religion the support rests on the side of a "positive exclusivism"—that is, a loving but affirmative support of the uniqueness of

God's action both in Israel of the Old Testament and the New Testament church. But more specifically for the Christian, the singularity of God's saving action in Jesus Christ is unique.

Within this chapter there emerges what one might term *a theology of exclusivism* which undergirds the calling of Israel as the people of God (vv. 6-11). The uniqueness of Israel rested in her position as a holy people, separated for the Lord (v. 6), the power of God's love in life (v. 7), the promises of God to the patriarchs (v. 8, cf. Gen. 12:1 ff.), and the personality of the Lord as one who is faithful and who keeps covenant (vv. 9-10). Because of the uniqueness of Israel's relationship to the Lord, a unique performance was demanded of them: "You shall therefore be careful to do the commandment" (v. 11).

The rewards of exclusivism focus on the inward reality of covenant love and faithfulness (v. 12). But they also include external manifestations of love and blessing, reflected in the productivity of the created order (vv. 13-14), the assurances of health and well-being (v. 15), and triumph over national enemies (v. 16).

It was through the holy war that exclusivism was implemented (vv. 17-26). In response to the question of how Israel could dispossess the people in the land (v. 17), the answer came in assurances grounded in the memory of what God had done in the Exodus event. In the holy war the Lord had fought the battles of Israel, despite the fact that tribesmen themselves went to battle. So with the conquest there grew the conviction that "the LORD your God is in the midst of you, a great and terrible God" (v. 21). In response to the dispossession of the Canaanites, Israel was commended to eradicate all traces of "heathen" worship (vv. 25-26).

Is it possible to maintain the exclusive claims of biblical religion in the contemporary world without becoming rigid and hostile toward others who hold views other than one's own? Hopefully believers can maintain the uniqueness and conviction of their religious commitment, while affirming both its singularity in the midst of pluralism in religion and compassionate love toward all persons.

One God—One Source of Life (8:1-20)

According to Deuteronomy, *the discipline of the desert* came in order that Israel might learn "that man does not live by bread alone" (v. 3). Such trials as they experienced tested Israel "to know what was in your heart" (v. 2). Out of the travail of their experiences they perceived that the meaning of life is bound up in the power of God. Against the background of the discipline of the desert, *the desirability of the land* was all the more attractive (vv. 6-10). There were three conditions for experiencing the blessing of God: keeping his commandments, walking in his ways, and fearing him (v. 6). But despite the blessing of the land (vv. 7-9) and the consequences of God's blessing in one's life (v. 10), Israel also confronted *the danger of forgetting the One God* (vv. 11-20).

In a passage whose spirit is reminiscent of 6:10-15, Moses again cautioned Israel concerning the danger of forgetting the Lord. Pride and self-exaltation lead persons to forget their ultimate dependence on the Lord: "Then your heart be lifted up, and you forget the LORD" (v. 14). For those who succumb to that temptation, God's grace is ignored as the source of blessing (vv. 14-16). They are confused about the source of life's blessing (vv. 17-18), believing that "my power and the might of my hand have gotten me this wealth" (v. 17). The consequences of self-exaltation at the expense of God are clear. Such persons forfeit life (v. 19) and ultimately experience destruction (v. 20). Is it not logical to assume that if there is only one God, there is only one source of life for humanity? Only in him was life in the beginning; only in him is there life now; only in him shall there be life hereafter. For the Lord is the singular, unique, and only God.

One God—One Source of Success (9:1 to 10:11)

The word "success" is so abused in contemporary society by the superficial ways in which it is used to assess life that one hesitates to refer to it in connection with this biblical theme. But in its finest, most splendid sense, success is not only humanity's desire but God's purpose. No one wants persons to succeed in life any more than God. And success is more crucial for living in its totality than for many of the isolated experiences that each person often overvalues. This theme is developed in Deuteronomy along two lines: the statement of a principle (vv. 1-7) and the illustration of that principle (9:8 to 10:11).

The principle enunciated was twofold. *First,* the one God prepares the way for his people (9:1-3). Success in life is more often than not dependent upon events over which persons have had no control. In this instance, Israel was to cross the Jordan and confront those people who had prevented them from entering Kadesh over forty years earlier. How could they now succeed when previously they had failed? The answer is clear and direct: "Know therefore this day that he who goes over before you . . . is the LORD your God" (9:3). As has been true to this day, success within the covenant community is more dependent on the preparatory work of God who goes before than it is upon either individual or collective characteristics of God's people.

Second, success is due to God, not to persons. The conquest succeeded because of God's judgment on the people of the land (9:4-5a) and because God was fulfilling the covenant word he swore to Abraham (9:5b). Success also came despite Israel's rebellions, not because of her fidelity (9:6-7).

As though to illustrate that the success of the covenant depended on God and not Israel, Moses illustrated this by beginning with the faithlessness of Israel at Sinai in the making of the golden calf, then tracing their rebellions through the wilderness wanderings (9:8 to 10:11). By this technique he sought to demonstrate that the transcendent power in human life rests with God. The future of the covenant rests in God and what he does, despite rebellious persons who serve him imperfectly. Since there is only one God, there is only one source of success in life.

One God—One Ultimate Relationship (10:12-22)

Persons are involved in multiple relationships, each encircling the other like a series of concentric circles—some larger and some smaller in their significance for one's life. Although few rank their relationships with other persons and institutions by levels of importance, such an exercise is possible. One could rank all of life's relationships. What constitutes the largest of the concentric circles, embracing all other relationships? Jesus put it this way: "But seek first his kingdom and his righteousness, and all these things shall be yours as well" (Matt. 6:33). Since there is only one God, the ultimate relationship in life is that which you experience with the Lord.

Within that relationship, what does the Lord require? Deuteronomy lists commitments. *First,* there is the requirement to honor God through fearing him, walking in his ways, loving him, serving him, and by keeping his Commandments (vv. 12-13). In each of these five ways one may honor God in a manner consistent with a relationship that is ultimate.

Second, one is to submit to God (vv. 14-16). Israel was called to circumcise their hearts as opposed to the traditional foreskin. They were to remove anything that obscured the heart from the reality of God's word, opening the heart to the presence of God. Such action was grounded in the sovereignty of God, for to him belong all things (v. 14). Also, the Lord's grace in choosing Israel prompted such submission of the heart to God, rejecting stubbornness as a quality of relationship. As Paul later challenged the church at Rome, "I appeal to you . . . by the mercies of God" (Rom. 12:1).

Third, if one's relationship with God is of ultimate significance, he is required to imitate God (vv. 17-19). The narrative begins with a graphic description of God as *sovereign* (v. 17*a*), *mighty* (v. 17*b*), *impartial* (v. 17*c*), and *just* toward the helpless (v. 18). But how does the characterization of God define the quality of human response? Having described who God is and how he relates to others, then the author addresses Israel: "Love the sojourner therefore" (v. 19). This means that you are to be like God, imitating his love and justice (v. 19).

Fourth, out of the context of a person's ultimate relationship with God, he is to be grateful to God (vv. 20-22). The word gratitude does not appear, but the text does state that "He is your praise" (v. 21); and in the psalms Israel praised God for his goodness far more than they thanked him in the modern sense of thanksgiving. Four actions reveal that God is a person's praise: fear the Lord, serve him, cleave to him, and swear by his name (v. 20).

One God—One Fundamental Choice (11:1-32)

There is one fundamental choice for those who believe that there is only one God: obedience or disobedience. In this chapter the writer discusses the obligations of obedience, the motives for obedience, and the contrasts between obedience and disobedience.

What is the threefold obligation of obedience? If one does respond positively to the Lord, what is required? The phrase "you shall therefore" occurs three times (vv. 1,8,18) and divides verses 1-25 into three logical and coherent elements. "You shall therefore love the LORD your God" (v. 1). This is established at the outset as the primary responsibility within covenant relationships. There is much unclear thinking about the Old Testament, especially with regard to law and grace, love and wrath—as though the Old Testament knew nothing of grace

and love. Nothing could be further from the truth. Even in the case
of the law, the covenant preceded law; and the stipulations of the
covenant expressed through law flowed out of the relationships initiated by God's grace. Love is the foundation on which all else rests.
Paul grasped this clearly in his observation that "love is the fulfilling
of the law" (Rom. 13:10). When Jesus isolated the great commandment
in the law, he joined two Old Testament passages: "You shall love
the LORD your God with all your heart, and with all your soul, and
with all your mind . . . And a second is like it, You shall love your
neighbor as yourself. On these two commandments depend all the
law and the prophets" (Matt. 22:37-40). Those two commandments
on which Jesus placed "all the law and the prophets" had appeared
earlier in the Shema of Deuteronomy 6:4-5 and in Leviticus 19:18.

"You shall therefore keep all the commandment" (vv. 8-17) formed
another obligation for covenant living. The Commandments were
given to Israel as guides to enable them to live out in life the demands
of the relationship created by the covenant. But the relationship was
prior to the Commandments (cf. Ex. 20:2; Deut. 5:6), for the Ten
Words were addressed to a redeemed community. Yet the relationship
did impose its demands, as do all relationships. It was those demands
or stipulations which formed the essence of the law.

Yet another obligation is equally clear: "You shall therefore lay up
these words of mine in your heart" (v. 18). Believers are to live out
of the Word of God, responding to the dynamic quality of God's creative, redeeming power in their lives. Such dynamism and creativity
as characterizes the Word suggest that there are no conditions within
the human situation which are outside the bounds of the dynamic
Word. So the obligations related to the demand for obedience are
clear. Believers are to love the Lord, keep his commandments, and
treasure his Word.

What are the motives for obedience? These appear in three sections
(vv. 1-8,9-17,18-25). Believers are to obey the command of God because of *discipline in history* (vv. 1-8). As the biblical writer suggests:
"Consider the discipline (or, instruction) of the LORD" (v. 2). God
teaches believers through historical events; the disciplined person (i.e.,
disciple) will learn from history that one should respond positively
to the Lord. As illustrations of that principle, Moses cited the Exodus
out of Egypt (vv. 3-4), the experiences of the wilderness (v. 5), and
the fate of those who disobeyed the Lord (v. 6). But most of all he

appealed to "all the great work of the LORD which he did" (v. 7).

Also, *the blessing of the land* formed another motive for obedience (vv. 8-17). Throughout these verses it is clear that fidelity to the Lord was clearly related to possessing the land (v. 8), living a long time in the land (v. 9), and the goodness of the land (vv. 10-12), as well as rain in its season (v. 14) and grass for the fields (v. 15). However a modern-day person may illustrate the principle the truth remains: There is an indelible linkage which one may trace between fidelity to the Lord and the good life for which persons seek.

Further, *the conquest of the land* was also related to covenant fidelity: "For if you will be careful to do all this commandment which I command you to do, loving the LORD your God, walking in all his ways, and cleaving to him, then the LORD will drive out all these nations before you" (vv. 22-23; cf. vv. 18-25).

The contrast between obedience and disobedience are clarified in terms of curse and blessing (vv. 26-32). The biblical concept of curse is more significant than contemporary profanity. It focuses on the concept of the word as dynamic, with the power of its own fulfillment. Blessings spoken would surely come to pass, for they possessed within the word(s) the power of fulfillment. So also with cursing; and it was for this reason that the Old Testament condemned so strongly the cursing of a deaf person. Since one could not hear, he would not know that a curse had been placed on him; nor could he take action against the curse (cf. Lev. 19:14).

So the alternatives for Israel, as for every generation, were clear: Blessing or cursing, which would one choose? Later the covenant renewal ceremony pictured an extended development of this brief introduction to cursing and blessing. For there one discovers an extended statement of curses (27:11-26) and blessings (28:1-6). Thus the alternatives for life are clear: a life cursed in the primitive sense of disaster, trial, and purposelessness, or life blessed of God in ways so richly described throughout the Bible.

In summary, the whole of Deuteronomy 5—11 focuses on the character of God (chap. 5) and the conduct of man (chaps. 6—11). The latter section is essentially a commentary on the First Commandment. Since there is only one God, then there flows from this singular and unique relationship responsibilities which are to characterize the conduct of man. There is to be one faithful fellowship (chap. 6), one people of God (chap. 7), one source of life (chap. 8), one source of success (9:1 to 10:11), one ultimate relationship (10:12-22), and one fundamental choice (chap. 11).

The Demands of Covenant Living
12:1 to 26:19

What does it mean to be the people of God, living in covenant relationship with him and with other persons? To a significant degree, this question may be answered by our examining the legal section of Deuteronomy (12—26). Here the writer collected laws appropriate to defining the nature of covenant expectations. Often Old Testament laws have been interpreted as negative, burdensome impositions on human freedom. But such an interpretation, even in the New Testament, often was much more influenced by the perversion of the law in later Judaism than by an understanding of the relationship of covenant and law in early Israel. For the law was not a personal burden to be borne, not as God provided it as covenant stipulations in the beginning of Israel's covenant experience. Rather, the law was like a light guiding Israel to embody in history what covenant relationships implied for personal and corporate living.

It would be impossible within the limitations of space imposed for this study to consider each stipulation in isolation or in great detail. How then can we study such an extensive collection of laws? *First,* we might isolate different themes for the broad areas within the legal section. *Second,* within those larger areas we may develop subsidiary themes. Then we would have a reasonably clear understanding of the major concerns of the legal section and could turn to special studies of Deuteronomy to study individual laws with greater detail. Following this pattern, within the fifteen chapters of the legal section, it is possible to isolate seven basic demands for covenant living: purity in worship (12:1 to 17:7), acknowledging authority (17:8 to 18:22), justice in criminal cases (19:1-21), humanitarian conduct in warfare (20:1 to 21:14), morality in conduct (21:1 to 25:18), responsibility in worship and social concern (26:1-15), and fidelity to the covenant (26:16-29). Throughout these sections there is a consistent emphasis on exhortation, appealing to Israel to embody the stipulations on covenant living. In Deuteronomy the law is more than a mere listing or codification. It is an urgent, moving appeal which exhorts people to respond. Simply stated, it is preached law.

Preaching on Purity of Worship (12:1 to 17:7)

As stressed throughout the book of Leviticus, holiness was central both to Old Testament worship and to Old Testament life. Because God was "wholly other" than persons or places, persons were to worship him in ways that reflected that holiness. God could be approached only at particular places and in prescribed ways.

Covenant living affirms that worship is central for a person's life and that it is consistent with the nature and character of God. It should be no surprise, therefore, that the first concern for covenant living focuses on worship (12:1 to 17:7). Four themes are central to the Deuteronomic concern for the purity of worship: the holiness of worship (12—13), the holiness of worshipers (14:1-21), the holiness of worship structures (14:22 to 17:1), and the fate of the apostate [as an exhortation to holiness] (17:2-7).

The Holiness of Worship (12:1 to 13:18)

Both *the place of worship* (12:1-28) and *the person worshiped* (12:29 to 13:18) are crucial to dynamic worship. Although persons worshiped in the home and at local shrines throughout the history of Israel, there came a time when Israel sought to centralize worship at Jerusalem. This was directly related to the reform movement of Josiah in the seventh century B.C. and is the probable intent of Deuteronomy: "You shall seek the place which the LORD your God will choose out of all your tribes to put his name and make his habitation" (v. 5). Permission was granted for the ritual slaughter of animals in areas far removed from the central sanctuary (vv. 15-28), and persons scattered in exile were cautioned about fidelity to the Lord (vv. 29-31). But the priority of the central place of worship remained clear.

So for modern persons, the concentration of public worship in a "central sanctuary" continues to be both positive and necessary. Although few today would call for a return to the legal stipulations related to Jerusalem as the single sanctuary for sacrifice and offerings, most believers affirm the priority of a place of worship. *Place* is not unimportant, and it is meaningful that one shares common worship with the community of believers. The sanctity of the place of worship is a continuing and vital aspect both of worship and nurture in covenant faith.

More important than the place of worship was *the holiness of the One worshiped* (13:1-18). Above all else, covenant living implies that one maintains the uniqueness of the Lord, that he both acknowledges his holiness for himself and affirms that for the community. The previous chapter closed with a warning against apostasy (12:29-32), followed in chapter 13 by a discussion of three categories of persons who may lead others astray. These may compromise one's dedication to the Holy One of Israel: religious leaders (vv. 1-5), family (vv. 6-11), and citizens of your cities (vv. 12-18).

Persons may be led away from faith into apostasy (in the Old Testament sense) by *religious leaders.* Israel was warned that if a prophet rises and says, "Let us go after other gods" (v. 2), the people were not to listen. Members of the covenant community are obliged to weigh carefully the teaching of religious leaders. Although contemporary leaders are more often than not characterized by responsible theological and ethical leadership, there are exceptions. "You shall not listen to the words of that prophet" (v. 3). Religious leadership should be tested against the authenticity of the Lord's revelation within the covenant community.

Even *family members* may mislead one by influencing other members of the family to abandon the Lord (vv. 6-11). Regardless of such family relationship (v. 6), one should not listen: "You shall not yield to him or listen to him" (v. 8).

Often *community opinion* may lead a person to compromise faith, convincing him to substitute an understanding of the community or the cultural and social concepts of the era for a living relationship with the Lord.

The holiness of worship may be protected well in every generation by, *first,* assuring a holy place of worship; *second,* refusing to be led away from covenant faith by religious leaders, members of a person's family, or community pressure. How much more vibrant Christian commitment would be for many persons today if these principles were implemented in contemporary society.

The Holiness of Worshipers (14:1-21)

A person reflects his relationship with God through a unique life-style. Some animals were prohibited because they are flesh which had not been ritually slaughtered. In some instances animals may have been revered in other worship systems. Dietetic implications may have been involved. But what is most important is not the ultimate rationale for rejecting some animals as food. The most significant aspect of these ritual prescriptions focused on the fact that through abstaining from eating those animals, Israelites manifested to whom they belonged. By refusing foods incompatible with the holiness of God, they retained their relationship with the Lord. Such views were primitive, to be sure, and few today would insist on literally implementing such laws. But in principle they may still be affirmed with integrity. Persons in relationship with the Lord are to maintain the sanctity of that fellowship.

Fundamental to this chapter is the uniqueness of Israel. Such uniqueness was affirmed through a unique relationship with the Lord: "You are the sons of the LORD your God" (v. 1). On that fundamental presupposition the remainder of the chapter rests. The fact that you are people of God imposes its own set of demands. How then was that uniqueness to find expression? The answer is clear: by avoiding pagan mourning rites (vv. 1-2), unclean foods (vv. 3-21), and pagan ritual (v. 21*b*).

The Holiness of Worship Structures (14:22 to 16:22)

To maintain the purity of worship, it is also necessary to preserve worship structures. The way in which one worshiped in the Old Testament was far less important for later biblical religion; but throughout the Bible and into contemporary society, the way in which one worships is not unimportant.

Although the structures cited in Deuteronomy are not all-inclusive, they reflect excellent principles. *First*, the structure of worship provided for the dedication of one's possessions (14:22 to 15:23). Whether in the giving of tithes (14:22-29), granting release to all that were bound through indebtedness or other forms of servitude (15:1-18), or dedicating the firstborn to the Lord, persons confronted unique opportunities in worship for giving dynamic expression to their faith.

Whatever the era, a person gives himself through giving his possessions. Biblical religion continues to affirm freedom from all forms of
bondage as in the year of release. And the commitment of succeeding
generations continues to be an area of significant concern in the worship experience. *Second,* the dedication of life was also achieved
through an annual calendar of festival celebration: Passover (16:1-
8), Pentecost (16:9-12), and Tabernacles (16:13-17). In these celebrative moments in the worshiping community, persons recalled the historical dimension of their religious pilgrimage. They affirmed the
goodness of God's gift of earth and productivity, and they praised
God for his providence which had brought them through sea and
wilderness. Such moments make of worship both proclamation and
response: proclaiming what God has done and making appropriate
response to his gracious action in one's pilgrimage.

Third, justice was also an integrated component for Israel as a worshiping community. At the conclusion of this narrative which focuses
on the festivals, the editor of the book added a call to justice (vv.
18-20). Judges were to be appointed in all towns (v. 18), and persons
were not to pervert justice by showing partiality or by taking a bribe
(v. 19). The ideal is clear: "Justice, and only justice, you shall follow"
(v. 20).

In summary, how does a person maintain the holiness of worship
structures? He dedicates himself through his possessions; he proclaims
and responds to God's gracious gifts during celebrative moments of
the year. One incorporates justice for all persons into the fabric of
one's community, for that too is a form of worship.

The Fate of the Apostate (17:1-7)

The exhortation to purity of worship also gave attention to the
apostate, that person or those persons in Israel who abandoned the
Lord for other gods. The seriousness of abandoning the Lord was
clearly implied in the death penalty prescribed for such offenses (vv.
5-7). Although no one is likely to suggest the death penalty for religious
infidelity, the fact that Israel did do this underscores the seriousness
of the issue despite the contemporary rejection of the penalty. The
point is clear. One cannot maintain purity of worship if the community
of faith is eroded by persons committed to other gods. Stated positively, contemporary persons exemplify the demands of the covenant

through fidelity to covenant stipulations and by living in relationship to the Lord.

Preaching on Authority (17:8 to 18:22)

A second demand for covenant living is to acknowledge authority. Relationship to authority and to authority figures is a troubling issue with which many persons struggle but never resolve satisfactorily. Although there was no effort to suppress the integrity of personal initiative and responsibility, the biblical revelation does affirm the propriety of authority structures. In this instance Deuteronomy affirms the integrity of government (17:8-20; cf.16:18-20), the equality and support of religious leadership (18:1-8), and the validity of prophetic witness (18:9-22).

The Integrity of Government (17:8-20)

The integrity of government rests, *first*, on the principle of justice. Such a principle is fundamental to the juristic system. Both ancient and modern courts exist for the purpose of assuring justice throughout the land. The desire that justice prevail for all persons was a constant concern in Israel (cf. 16:18-20).

Second, the principle of arbitration and obedience is crucial to the juristic system. Deuteronomy provided for the submission of difficult cases to a central court (vv. 8-9), but only in those instances in which justice could not be achieved at the local level (cf. 16-18). The reference in verse 8 to "the place which the LORD your God will choose" likely means Jerusalem (cf. Deut. 12:5). When this "court of appeal" had given its verdict, obedience was required (vv. 10-13). "Then you shall do according to what they declare to you from that place" (v. 10).

Third, government is epitomized in the choice of a king, but even the king was subordinate to God (vv. 14-20). This passage attempts to meld the concept of monarchy and theocracy. Kingship is permitted (vv. 14-15), but specific stipulations were given to control that form of government.

The integrity of government may be assured through the principle of justice, the acceptance of arbitration in cases of disagreement, and subordination of kingship to the Lord.

The Equality and Support of Religious Leaders (18:1-8)

While considering the role of authority in the community of faith, it is logical to turn, as did the writer, to religious leadership. In Israel such leadership was far more powerful than for contemporary persons in the free church tradition. *First,* the Levites were assured of a continuing right to physical support (vv. 1-5). It is highly probable that this passage addresses one of the problems created when the local shrines were displaced by the central sanctuary, with an attendant displacement of Levitical priests of the North. There is an obligation for the community of faith to care appropriately for such ministers.

Second, the equality of the priests suggests that rural Levitical priests displaced from their local places of service with the centralization of worship were entitled to minister at the Jerusalem Temple (vv. 6-8). The text is clear; there was to be no discrimination within the ministry. A Levitical priest coming from the most obscure rural village had a legitimate right to minister in the name of the Lord at the Jerusalem Temple (v. 7). Such equality in any generation could creatively advance the positive ministry of God's servants; yet one wonders whether contemporary persons take seriously this call to ministerial equality.

The Validity of the Prophetic Word (18:9-22)

The third area of authority addressed as an area of demand for covenant living was the issue of divine revelation. How can one know the revelation of God? *First,* the uniqueness of that revelation from the Lord led to the *condemnation of pagan religious practices* (vv. 9-14). As the faith community searches for the basis of ultimate authority, we may be sure that it does not rest in systems and practices which stand over against the Lord and covenant commitment. There is an exclusivism about biblical faith which excludes pagan religious practices.

Second, continuity in divine revelation was affirmed in the promise that the Lord will raise up "a prophet like me" (v. 15) [i.e., Moses] who will bear the words of God.

Third, the *compulsive power of the prophetic word* (vv. 19-20) was such that it commanded obedience from those who heard (v. 18). It also decreed destruction for false prophets who pretended to speak the word of the lord but who spoke their own words (v. 19).

Fourth, the *content of the prophetic word* was the test of its authenticity (vv. 21-22). Did its content come to pass? Was content consistent with performance? These criteria are continuing tests for the validity of the prophetic word. But the implication is also clear that only if the word is the Lord's is one obliged to hear. Only if it is the word of the false prophet may one reject the word—and this on the basis that "the prophet has spoken it presumptuously, you need not be afraid of him" (v. 20).

Preaching on Justice

The concern for justice in the Old Testament focused not only on general principles within the community but especially on criminal cases. Every effort was expended to assure that justice was implemented, with equality both to the accused and to the victim. Efforts were made to protect persons from intemperate wrath (vv. 1-13), to protect property rights (v. 14), and to protect an accused person against a false witness (vv. 15-21).

Protecting Persons Against Intemperate Wrath (19:1-13)

The cities of refuge were designed as places to which persons who had killed another, whether deliberately or accidentally, might take refuge until the case might be decided. Intrinsic to the problem was the principle of blood revenge. Should a person be killed, for whatever reason, the nearest of kin to the deceased was obliged to avenge the blood of his kinsman. It was against intemperate wrath that the cities were established as a haven of safety. For example, "anyone [who] kills his neighbor unintentionally . . . as when a man goes into the forest with his neighbor to cut wood, and his hand swings the axe . . . and the head slips from the handle and strikes his neighbor so that he dies" (vv. 4-5) could find refuge. But if a murderer (v. 11) found refuge, once the case was decided, the elders of the city handed him over to the avenger of blood (v. 12). Yet the principle is clear in either instance: People of God are obliged to protect persons against intemperate wrath.

Respecting Property Rights (19:14)

In a single verse which interrupts the larger discussion of justice, the obligation to protect property rights was included within the responsibilities of the covenant community. Persons should be able to hold property without fear of theft or intimidation, as suggested in both the eighth and the tenth of the Ten Words.

Protecting Persons Against False Witnesses (19:15-21)

That the false witness was a common problem throughout the Old Testament era may be illustrated by the numerous ways in which the problem was constantly addressed. An accused person was protected from the false charges of a malicious witness in two ways. *First,* "a single witness shall not prevail against a man for any crime" (v. 15). A person could be convicted only on the evidence of multiple witnesses. *Second,* a most interesting law developed to discourage the malicious witness. In disputed cases in which the witness was proven to be a malicious witness, "you shall do to him as he had meant to do to his brother" (v. 19). To illustrate, should one be on trial for a crime involving the death penalty, a false witness was put to death. If implemented, such a procedure might do much to create integrity with witness in law courts both ancient and modern. Also, it should be noted that it was in this context that one of the Old Testament references to "eye for eye, tooth for tooth, hand for hand, foot for foot" emerged. Although more often than not condemned and caricatured as "less than Christian" by many, the passage has positive contextual significance. To assure integrity in the courts, one should do to the witness as he had intended to do to the accused.

Preaching on Humanitarian Conduct of War (20:1-20; 21:10-14)

On first examination, to speak of the humanitarian conduct of a war may appear altogether inconsistent. But historically war has been subject to general limitations because of humanitarian concerns. In ancient Israel the holy war was central to the conquest, and the specific stipulations governing its conduct are instructive for understanding the humanitarian concern which characterized such a war.

Conscription of Men for War (20:1-9)

First, the *conscription of men for warfare* embodied specified exemptions from military service (vv. 1-9). Persons who had built a new house (v. 5) but had not dedicated it; who had planted a vineyard but had not enjoyed its fruit (v. 6); or who had betrothed a wife but had not consummated the marriage (v. 7) were exempt from military service.

Conciliatory Efforts Toward the Enemy (20:10-18)

Second, conciliatory efforts should be made toward an enemy prior to launching an attack (vv. 10-18). Not only should one make overtures of peace prior to battle (vv. 10-11), but mercy should be extended toward distant cities (vv. 12-15). In contrast to distant cities, however, those within the area given to Israel were to be exterminated according to the guidelines of holy war (vv. 16-18). Although the norms were not altogether ideal from the perspective of later biblical revelation, the emphasis on conciliation remains a worthy goal.

Consideration for the Countryside (20:19-20)

Third, consideration for the countryside was to be maintained (vv. 19-20). Here we discover a primitive ecology: Trees were not to be cut down. "You may eat of them, but you shall not cut them down" (v. 19). The only exception to this was the nonfruitbearing trees. They could be cut to build seige works (v. 20). Knowing that the populace depended on the fruit trees, Israel was forbidden to destroy them during warfare.

Procedures for an Unsolved Murder (21:1-9)

The entire sacrificial procedure to gain forgiveness for an unsolved murder is different from the usual Israelite procedure. The killing of the sacrifice did not take place at the tabernacle. There was nothing said of what to do with the blood of the sacrifice. This particular sacrifice seems to be a very old sacrificial procedure taken over by Israel upon moving into Canaan.

At least the reason for the sacrifice seems clear. Murder made the land unclean. True worship could not be maintained in an unclean land. This unusual sacrifice procedure was carried out to gain forgiveness for the blood guilt of the unknown murderer. Verse 9 seems to be a formula showing the right way to please God. The formula may be seen in 13:5; 17:7; 19:13.

Captive Women and Human Dignity (21:10-14)

Fourth, captive women were to be treated respectfully (21:10-14). The abuse of women has been a historical embarrassment during war, even in recent wars of the twentieth century. But note that in early Israel, if one saw among the captives a woman for whom one had desire, she was not to be molested. Rather, she was brought to one's home where she experienced purification rites (v. 12). Only then could the warrior *marry* her (v. 13), but with the reservation that "if you have no delight in her, you shall let her go where she will." Yet she could not be sold as a slave, "since you have humiliated her" (v. 14). For its era, such stipulations represented a marked sense of idealism for the treatment of women.

Preaching on Morality in Conduct (21:1-9,15 to 25:19)

The legal section which extends from chapter 21 through chapter 25 is composed of a wide variety of stipulations which focus on morality in conduct. Common life was regulated by divine law (21:1 to 22:12), and purity of sexual standards was to characterize the covenant community (22:13-30). Holiness necessary for God's presence was protected (23:1-14), and personal morality was governed by covenant stipulations (23:15 to 25:19).

Regulating Common Life by Divine Principles (21:1-9,15 to 22:12)

Although these stipulations are widely varying in content, they have an integrating focus in the effort to regulate corporate life by divine law. That the whole of corporate life was a concern for covenant faith is suggested in areas of concern as widely varying as the expiation necessary for an unsolved murder, which assumes corporate responsibility (21:1-2); the inheritance rights of persons (21:15-17); or the worthless son who disgraced his parents (21:18-21). There was even a stipulation on removing the body of an executed criminal, lest one accursed by God defile the land; and hanging on the tree was a symbol of divine curse (21:22-23).

But at the more personal level, laws reflected concern for one's neighbor (22:1-12), and lost property was to be returned to the owner

(22:1-3). One was to volunteer assistance to a neighbor in need (22:4); and even animals were to be protected, as in the case of a bird and its young (22:6-7). Persons had responsibility for others, and one building a house with a flat roof was obliged to build a parapet on the roof (22:8). Even ways of dress were prescribed, as was the general impropriety of mixing incompatible items of dress or other objects (22:5,9-11).

Protecting the Purity of Sexual Standards (22:13-30)

In the covenant community, every effort was taken to maintain purity of sexual standards. Although specific applications may appear far removed from twentieth-century life the principles abide. The community of faith should be concerned for sexual purity, and churches have an imperative responsibility to address this most personal of relationships. For example, accusations concerning chastity (vv. 13-21) exemplify the ideal of sexual purity. Although one would hardly infer the same procedure in dealing with sexual promiscuity (cf. vv. 15-17), nor would one call for a return to the public whipping of the man guilty of promiscuity (v. 18), the ethical idealism of the law is commendable. Other areas of sexual life such as adultery (vv. 22), the seduction of a virgin (vv. 23-29), and incest, probably involving one's stepmother (v. 30), together underscore the demand for sexual purity as a continuing characteristic for the persons living out of the demands of covenant faith.

Protecting One's Relationship with the Lord (23:1-14)

As often emphasized in Leviticus, Numbers, and Deuteronomy, the holiness necessary for the presence of God in the covenant community was guarded through a variety of intricate and primitive procedures. Here the same theme reappears. For example, certain persons were excluded from the assembly of the Lord, lest their condition violate that holiness. Such persons included the eunuch (v. 1), the bastard (v. 2), and those who prevented Israel from passing through their territory during the wilderness pilgrimage (vv. 3-6). Also, within the military camp holiness was protected from the uncleanness of bodily discharges (vv. 10-14).

Again specific laws have been subsumed by the fuller revelation of God. But the principle of maintaining a holy community appropriate to the presence of God remains valid even today.

Personal Morality and Conduct (23:15 to 25:19)

Within this collection of stipulations there are at least nineteen areas addressed. These include refuge for escaped slaves (vv. 15-16), the categorical rejection of sexual irregularity (vv. 17-18), interest on loans (vv. 19-20), and keeping one's word (vv. 21-23). A person was permitted to use a neighbor's crop to satisfy human hunger (vv. 24-25).

Marriage was also a relationship of concern, as in prohibiting the remarriage of a divorced wife (24:1-4) or in the exemption of the newly married from the army or "any business" (24:5). Concern for the needs of families was reflected in the fact that one's mill and upper millstone were exempt from pledges for debts (24:6). Israelite slavery was prohibited (24:7). The priests of Israel were in charge of caring for diseases that made people unclean. Leprosy was such a disease (vv. 8-9). Compare Leviticus 13—14. The story of Miriam was a historical reminder (Num. 12:9 ff.). Pledges or collateral taken for loans were both collected, used, and returned in such manner to respect human dignity (24:10-13). A hired servant was not to be oppressed (24:14-15), and there was to be no corporate punishment for individual crimes (24:16). Helpless persons were to be assisted (24:17-22), and limitations were placed on punishment (25:1-3). Care was given to work animals (25:4). Laws regulated the marriage of a brother's widow (25:5-10). Immodest assault on another person was prohibited, but probably more for the religious overtones of sexuality than for immodesty (25:11-12). One was to be honest in trading, using appropriate units of weights and measures (25:13-16).

A marked difference appears in this part of Deuteronomy (vv. 17-19). Exodus 17:8-16 is the historical backdrop for this "remembrance of Amalek" that the writer called Israel not to forget.

Although efforts to legislate either public or private morality inevitably fail, the idealism remains. Through appropriate ethical and theological guidelines, the covenant community is to exalt personal morality and conduct.

Preaching on Worship and Social Concern (26:1-15)

Someone once observed that every religion must have a system of ideas, pattern of ethics, and a means to achieve the joy of salvation.

Each of these three factors is embedded in this chapter. It contains one of the earlier theological statements on the nature of God's relationship to Israel and is a summation of what Israel believed about God's action (vv. 5-10).

At least annually, during the offering of firstfruits, Israel declared her faith. She found in worship the opportunity to celebrate the joy of her salvation experienced through the mighty hand of God (v. 8). Also, the produce tithe was to be shared with the needy (vv. 12-15), calling Israel to an ethical commitment within covenant faith. What you believe about God, how you relate to other persons, and the way in which you celebrate the joy of salvation in worship are appropriate concerns for both ancient temple and temporary church.

Preaching on Covenant Fidelity (26:16-19)

The legal section of Deuteronomy closes with a brief exhortation to covenant fidelity. Although exceedingly brief, it is an appropriate conclusion to an emphasis on the demands of covenant living (12—26). Covenantal obligations are clear. Israel declared on that day that the Lord was her God, that she would keep his commandments and obey his voice (v. 17). The Lord also assumed responsibilities within the covenant relationship. He promised to make Israel his own possession, to set her above all others, and to make of them a holy people (vv. 18-19). The Lord will keep faith with the covenant stipulations, and a comparable obligation rests on Israel. Covenants involve dual responsibilities, and the legal section of Deuteronomy appropriately concludes with a reminder of those demands for covenant living.

Joys and Hardships of Following God
27:1 to 28:68

Following the legal section of Deuteronomy these chapters appropriately set before Israel the alternatives of cursing and blessing— cursing if the law was not maintained, blessing if the law was fulfilled.

Such an emphasis was consistent with the twofold focus on proclamation and exhortation throughout the book. Moses proclaimed the acts of God, then exhorted Israel to respond to God's revelation in history. So here the law was proclaimed, and Israel was challenged to respond positively to those covenant stipulations.

Renewing the Covenant (27:1-26)

The *first* requirement of covenant renewal for Israel was the publication of the law (vv. 1-8). After crossing the Jordan they were to set up stones on Mount Ebal, plaster them, and write the Lord's commandments (vv. 2-5,8). After publishing the law, the *second* stipulation in the covenant renewal ceremony was the formal oath of loyalty: "This day you have become the people of the LORD . . . You shall therefore obey the voice of the LORD your God, keeping his commandments" (vv. 9-10). *Third* in the ritual of renewal was the proclamation of the curses (vv. 11-26). Initially this passage may have contained both curses and blessings, but presently there are only curses; and these are distinct from those in 28:1-68. Some characterize this as a dodecalogue, containing twelve commandments set in the format of curses. These related to idolatry (v. 15); disrespect for parents (v. 16); dishonesty concerning property (v. 17); abuse of a blind man (v. 18); perverting justice (v. 19); sexual abberrations including incest, probably involving multiple marriages and a wife other than the child's blood mother (v. 20); bestiality (v. 21); sexual intercourse with one's sister, regardless of the mother (v. 22); sexual intercourse with one's mother-in-law (v. 23); the murder of a neighbor in secret (v. 24); bribery of an innocent person (v. 25); and failure to confirm the law by doing it (v. 26). This twelve-law list of commandments should be studied together with the decalogues of Exodus 20 and Deuteronomy 5 in examining Old Testament legal codes.

The Blessing and the Curse (28:1-68)

The Blessing of Obeying God (28:1-14)

In an extended category of blessings, the positive aspects of covenant fidelity were isolated for ancient Israel. It should be noted, *first,* that there was a *conditional* aspect to those blessings (v. 1). *Second,* the blessings were *comprehensive* in their scope and encompassed the whole of life (vv. 2-6). *Third,* the *content* of the blessings was equally comprehensive and touched on such areas of life as the defeat of one's enemies (v. 7); one's barns and all of one's endeavors (v. 8); the relationship of Israel to other people and to the Lord (vv. 9-10); the bounty of cattle, as well as the fruit of the ground (v. 11); rain in time of need (v. 12); and general national exaltation as long as the nation remained faithful to the Lord (vv. 13-14).

The Curse of Disobeying God (28:15-68)

The writer presupposed, *first,* that there was a *causal* relationship between disobedience and the curses experienced in life (v. 15). The *comprehensive* nature of the curse constituted a *second* element in the charge; whether one was in the city or the field (v. 16), all aspects of life would be cursed (vv. 18-19). *Third,* the *content* of the curses was clarified and included calamity in nature (vv. 20-24); conflict in war and its attendant horror (vv. 25-35); contradiction and reversal of the good (vv. 36-46); conquest and horrors of siege (vv. 47-57); as well as a general summary of other calamities (vv. 58-68).

As in ancient Israel, so in contemporary life—there is a blessing inherent in following the Lord with fidelity, just as there are attendant disasters for those who abandon the Lord. Persons may differ in the manner in which causal responsibility is traced for varying natural calamities, but covenant believers generally agree that there are inherent blessings in fellowship with the Lord. There is an equal barrenness of life apart from that communion.

Daily Dedication of Oneself to God
29:1 to 30:20

The third speech of Moses introduced an emphasis on covenant renewal. The covenant had been made at Sinai (29:1), but with the passage of time there was need for covenant renewal. Just as in contemporary life there remains the constant need to renew one's covenant relationships, so on the plains of Moab Moses led the Israelites to reaffirm their faith. But the passage here moved beyond Moab to include covenant renewal ceremonies which occurred following Israel's occupation of the land. Indeed, beyond the words of the text one hears a word that clamors for covenant renewal as an ongoing experience for the people of God. Again, the polarities of proclamation and exhortation were intertwined. Deuteronomy 29:1-15 forms a confessional statement of God's action in history, counterbalanced by a moving call to commitment and obedience (29:16 to 30:20). As suggested throughout the study of Deuteronomy, the book is one of preached law and general exhortation that the people live out of covenant relationships and their demands.

Confessing What God Has Done (29:1-15)

On what basis should one accept the stipulations of the covenant? The answer is clear: because of what God has done in one's life (vv. 1-8). *Second,* on the basis of what God did from Egypt to Moab (vv. 1-8): "Therefore be careful to do the words of this covenant" (v. 9). The basis for covenant fidelity remains unchanged, whatever the generation. Consider what the Lord has done in one's life; then respond to him against the background of that grace. For the relationships of the covenant always precede covenant stipulations, just as grace precedes law, even in ancient Israel. *Third,* as Israel stood on the threshold of the land promised so long ago to the patriarchs, Moses reminded them of the fulfillment of God's promises (vv. 10-15). God is faithful and demands a correlated quality of fidelity from those in covenant relationship.

Committing Oneself to Obedience (29:16 to 30:20)

Moses called Israel to renewed commitment in five distinct areas of life. *First,* there was to be *no hypocrisy within the covenant,* for persons were to be faithful to their relationships (29:16-28). In cases of such hypocrisy, "The LORD would not pardon him" (29:20). *Second,* remember the *mystery and the challenge of revelation* (29:29). Years ago a seminary professor observed to a class, "A little healthy agnosticism never hurt anyone." By this he sought to lead the class to recognize the mystery of God's being. So here, "The secret things belong to the LORD our God; but the things that are revealed belong to us and to our children." Live out the demands of the revelation which come so clearly. Then learn to live with the mystery of God, with whom some things remain bound in impenetrable mystery.

Third, covenant relationships demand that one *live with repentance and renewal* (30:1-10). Judgment is a reality of life which should lead sensitive persons to repentance (30:1-2). For such persons restoration is always a possibility, as is the renewal of their lives in the Lord (30:3-10). *Fourth,* covenant relationships demand that one *maintain an awareness of the nearness of the Word* (30:11-14). One need not ask "who will go up for us to heaven" (30:12) or "who will go over the sea" (30:13). For "the word is very near you . . . so that you can do it" (30:14). The Word of revelation is not an impossible dream, but a present reality: You can do it! *Fifth,* members of the covenant community *live with the constant awareness of man's ultimate choice* (30:15-20). And what is the ultimate choice? The choices of life and death, good and evil, are ultimate choices, probing the farthest reaches of human existence. Hear the Word of God: "See, I have set before you this day life and good, death and evil" (30:15).

There could be no finer note on which the book of Deuteronomy might close than this: an urgent and moving appeal for persons in covenant relationship with the Lord to renew their lives in covenant fidelity. The appeal addresses the ultimate issues of life and death. Before turning to the appendix to Deuteronomy, one might well hear the challenge to covenant fidelity: "I have set before you life and death, blessing and curse; therefore choose life, that you and your descendants may live, loving the LORD your God, obeying his voice, and cleaving to him; for that means life to you" (30:19-20). On this stands the whole of covenant relationships.

Appendixes and Historical Notes
31:1 to 34:12

Following the speeches of Moses there have been appended historical notes (31:1-30), poetry of the covenant (33:1-29), and even an account of the death of Moses (34:1-12). These diverse components of the book contribute measurably to an understanding of Moses' role for later generations in Israel, as for the whole of the faith community to this day.

The Relationship of Moses and Joshua (31:1-30)

The relationship of Moses and Joshua is clarified in order that the transition of power to Joshua might be unquestioned (31:1-30). In his closing words, given at the age of 120 (31:2), Moses challenged Israel to cross the Jordan and dispossess the people, knowing that the Lord had given both to Israel (31:5). But most importantly, they were to act, knowing that the Lord had gone before them (31:6).

Calling Joshua to himself, Moses instituted a seventh-year covenant ceremony designed to assure the renewing of covenant bonds (31:7-13). Joshua was then formally chosen as successor to Moses (31:14-23), and the law was placed in the ark (31:24-29), consummating the ritual of transition between Moses and Joshua.

The Song of Moses (32:1-43)

The song of Moses (32:1-43) is an extended poetic composition which probably originated following the entrance and settlement periods. The song celebrates the coming victory of God and probably dates from the period immediately prior to the exile or shortly thereafter. Although ascribed to Moses (31:30), it is more likely a song honoring him because of the prominence which he had in shaping Israel's destiny.

Moses' Instructions (32:44-52)

Interspersed between the song of Moses and the blessing of Moses are the commendation of the law for Israel (32:44-47) and a narrative which describes Moses' call to die on Mount Nebo (32:48-52).

The Blessing of Moses (33:1-29)

The blessing of Moses follows the pattern of the blessing given within the family prior to the death of the father. Moses is portrayed speaking the word of blessing to all in Israel (33:1-29). As suggested previously, the word of blessing had the power of its own fulfillment and set in motion powers for the good of the one receiving the blessing. The poem is one which first exalts the God who came from Sinai (v. 1), one who "loved his people" and who held those people in his hands (v. 3). It was the God who met Israel at Sinai who became king (v. 5) and ruled in Israel. Only then does the poem turn to the blessing of the tribal figures, giving to each in turn a blessing uniquely descriptive of the history of the tribe (cf. 6-18,20,22-24). The poem then closes with an exaltation of God: "There is none like God" (v. 26) who brings to Israel qualities of life characterized by security (v. 27), safety (v. 28), happiness and salvation (v. 29).

Moses' Death and Burial (34:1-12)

The death and burial of Moses (34:1-12) now forms the conclusion of the book. Despite Moses' achievements and stimulating victories, his must have been a disappointing experience. For he viewed the whole of the land given in fulfillment of God's promise to the fathers (vv. 1-4), but he never entered that land (vv. 5-8). His was the tragedy of the religious leader who leads others to an idealized promised land, but in his own life dies separated from the promises. Dying in Moab is a haunting possibility even for persons who have given their best, for there are times when not even one's best is good enough.

The closing paragraph of the book focuses on the choice of Joshua, who "was full of the spirit of wisdom" (v. 9). But the paragraph also remains as an epitaph on the majesty of Moses as a most unique religious leader who saw the face of God in common places of life, who experienced God with an immediacy best characterized as "face to face" (v. 10). From the birth narrative in Exodus to the death scene in Deuteronomy, there was "none like him" (v. 11).